Unders
Conversation

Learn the Words, Phrases and Grammar Spanish Speakers Use Everyday and Quickly Become One Yourself!

Joe Kozlowski

Table of Contents

Introduction

Welcome to **Understanding Spanish Conversation**! I first want to congratulate you for continuing your quest of learning the Spanish language and for choosing this book to help you on that quest. There is no greater pleasure than helping other people reach their goals and it was such a pleasure writing this book. I thank you for choosing it.

A great many people have spent a great deal of time studying the Spanish language only to find themselves lacking the ability to hold any type of meaningful conversation. And all this despite taking many classes, studying countless grammar books, working translation exercises as well as many other things. All of this work is put in and very little is taken away from it in terms of improved conversational ability. Of course this ends up causing a great deal of frustration. This book will streamline your learning so that you will be able to immerse yourself in everyday talk with much less frustration. You will then improve your Spanish much more quickly as there is no better way to learn any language than through immersion.

In this book, I will provide the necessary tools to start having more meaningful conversations than "Where's the bathroom?" and "My name is Bob." I will take concepts that we use in everyday English conversation and show you how it is verbalized by a Spanish speaking person through explanations and examples. These explanations are written to be as simple as possible, well supported by examples. And they are written from the perspective of the native English speaker, such as myself, in order to make everything easier to understand.

I've gone through the frustrations and heartache that other English speakers go through learning Spanish. There are many obstacles and barriers that I overcame just to start becoming functional in speaking the language. I want to help you avoid these same obstacles. I taught myself the language using many different resources. From these resources, I learned what worked and what didn't. I also learned how to simplify this information in order to apply it verbally and in a conversational setting. I will only use as much grammar as necessary so that you will more easily understand how to use it, as opposed to teaching rules that are difficult to understand and even harder to apply. Grammar is not the focus of this book. Just a better understanding of how Spanish speakers communicate concepts and ideas that are used in everyday English conversation. In other words, just the grammar needed to communicate. As I've said before, I have gathered this information from many different sources and simplified it to make it easier to digest. Now, wouldn't you rather learn from someone who has already gone through all of the same trials and tribulations that you are currently experiencing in order to reach your goals?

Learning and understanding these everyday concepts will make it easier for you to immerse yourself in the language, eventually speaking confidently with Spanish speakers in no time. You don't even need to understand every concept in the beginning. If you just learn a few per week and practice them, you will significantly improve your conversational ability before you even know it. You will continually gain more and more confidence as time goes on. This book will prove to be a valuable resource that you will continue going back to. I am absolutely certain about that. Nothing will help you speak another language more quickly than understanding how it is spoken. This book will get you there. And once you're there, the additional confidence will even get you to enjoy speaking more, which will only improve your Spanish speaking abilities.

This book has each concept listed in alphabetical order with most of them in English and a few of them in Spanish. It doesn't need to be read in any particular order. Some concepts are harder to grasp than others. You may not understand some of them depending on your skill level and that's OK. If you don't understand one concept, just move on to the next one. After improving your skill level, you can go back to the original concept that gave you difficulty, which may then become easier to learn and understand. And when you practice what you've learned, don't worry about making mistakes, it's all part of the process. We always learn from our mistakes. This is especially true when learning a new language. All you have to do is keep at it.

Now, without any further due, let's get started!

Again

There are a couple of stock phrases in Spanish for "again," *otra vez* and *de nuevo*. Both work well and either one can be used at your discretion. In other words, you can either say *Necessito que lo hagas de nuevo* or *Necessito que lo hagas otra vez*. Each is perfectly fine for "I need you to do it again."

Volver a plus the infinitive works well for "again" as well. *Vuelvo a hacerlo más tarde* translates to "I'm doing it again later." "You're eating lobster again today?" would be *¿Vuelves a comer langosta hoy?*

Ask

Two words handle "to ask" in Spanish. It all depends on what one is asking. Use *preguntar* when asking for information or for an answer to a question. Use *pedir* when asking for something as in making a request. In other words, you *preguntar* who won the game last night, but you *pedir* the waitress for a coffee.

As soon as

There are a few options for "as soon as" in Spanish. They are *en cuanto*, *apenas*, and *tan pronto como*. You can even use *cuando*. Keep in mind that these phrases all use the subjunctive mood, which is explained in detail later in this book. Let's take a look at a couple of examples. In the first example, "As soon as I have the time, we will go out for dinner" can be stated as *En cuanto yo tenga el tiempo, salimos para cenar. Apenas* works in that example as well. In another example, if I want to tell you that I will help you as soon as I am done eating, then I could say *Te ayudaré tan pronto como yo termine comer. Tan pronto como* is best used in the middle of the sentence while the other examples are best used in the beginning. However, *cuando* could have been placed equally well in any of the examples shown as you can use it whenever "when" in English would be used, including in place of "as soon as."

Back/Behind

There are two good options to use when one wants to say that one thing is "behind" or "in back of" something else. These options are *detrás* and *atrás.* When one object is directly behind another or in pursuit of it, use *detrás.* Look at the following examples:

El perro está detrás del carro.(The dog is behind the car.)
José está detrás de la casa.(Jose is in back of the house.)
¿Están escondiendo detrás de esta pared los niños?(Are the children hiding behind this wall?)

When you want to say that something is behind or in back of something in a general or vague sense, use *atrás,* as in the following examples:

El perro está atrás.(The dog is out back.)
Tu libro está atrás allá.(Your book is back there.)
No mires atrás.(Don't look back.)

One good rule to follow is to use *detrás* when *de* is needed and *atrás* when it is not. The one exception is when you want to say that something/someone is behind another upon arrival, as in coming later. For instance, when you arrive at a party and your friend Josh is ten minutes behind you, you may say *Josh está atrás de mí* since he is arriving at a later point in time and is not right on your heels. He is instead at an undetermined location some distance behind you.

To say that something is in the very back, *al fondo* is a helpful phrase to know. For instance, if you ask where the bathroom is and it is all the way in the back of the building where one can go no further, you may hear *al fondo*. Or if it is "all the way in the back on the left," maybe *al fondo a la izquierda*.

When referring to "back" as in "to return," *de regresso* and *de vuelta* will work and are interchangeable. Examples for both include:

*Estoy de regresso de trabajo.(I'm back from work.)
*Ella está de vuelta de la escuela.(She is back from school.)

And of course, when referring to back as in "the spine," use *la espalda*.

Become

One of the hardest concepts for English speakers to master is "to become" for which Spanish uses several different verbs, depending on context. There are several different ways where things can change into, or become, something different. Some are more permanent and some are more sudden.   Each are expressed in different ways.

Ponerse, for example, would be used in fleeting, more temporary changes, such as emotions and feelings. Examples include *Me pongo enojado* for "I become angry." *Se pone borracho* for "He becomes drunk." *Te pones enfermo* for "You become sick."

When referring to longer-term changes that are much less reversible, use *hacerse*. So if you restore old houses someone may say *Estas casas se hacen bonitas cuando las arregulas.* Another example, "This restaurant is becoming popular" can be *Este restaurante se está haciendo popular.* It's also more likely used when change is intended. So if you start a business and *te haces rico,* your change to become rich was intended.

When you want to say "to turn out to be," *llegar a ser* works. For example*, Ayer por la tarde llegó a ser muy relajante* is "Yesterday afternoon turned out to be very relaxing." *Llegar a ser* can also be used for when someone becomes something in the sense of an accomplishment or that it took a lot of effort. *Veo que llegaste a ser medico* works for "I see that you became a doctor."

Volverse is used more for "to turn into," as in a more permanent but usually unexpected change. It's generally not something that is planned. To illustrate, if someone did not do well in school as a child but became very intelligent as an adult, you could say that *él se volvió inteligente.* It can also be used for a sudden, but longer lasting change in the way a lottery winner *se volvió rico.* It's the type of sudden change that will last for awhile if not forever.

For an even more complete change, *transformarse* and *convertirse* are used. Both are used to refer to a physical or an organic transformation, such as a caterpillar turning into a butterfly. Note the following examples:

Un niño se transforma en un hombre(A boy turns into a man).
El agua se transforma en hielo cuando hace muy frío en el invierno en Chicago(Water turns into ice when it is very cold in the winter in Chicago).
Clark Kent se convierte en Superman cada vez hay un crisis(Clark Kent turns into Superman each time there is a crisis).

Yet another way "to become" is to just take an adjective or a noun, make it reflexive and add an "a" or an "en" before it. For instance, *acercarse,* from *cerca,* would be used for "to become closer" and is used for "to approach." *Cuando se acerca a la escuela, hay un parque* works for "When one gets close to the school, there is a park." Look at the example with *frío. Mi café se enfria cuando lo bebo demasiado lentamente* is "My coffee becomes cold when I drink it too slowly." This way of conveying "to become" is commonly used in Spanish but often overlooked by those learning the language. Just take a couple of words and try it yourself.

Burn

This is not as simple in Spanish as it is in English. There are several verbs to use depending on the circumstance. *Quemar* is "to burn" as in to consume or damage by fire or heat when one thing burns another. For instance, the sun *quema* your skin, your friend always *quema* the food when he cooks, and your kid *quema* his finger on the stove. *Incendiar* is another choice for "to burn" but would be more specifically used for "to set on fire," usually for things that shouldn't be on fire in the first place such as houses, forests, clothing and so forth. So if a person throws gasoline on a house and lights it with a match, *él incendia la casa.* Once that person has lit the house on fire, the house itself is then burning. This "action of burning" is best covered by *arder.* So after someone *incendia la casa, la casa arde.* Another way to think of something that *arde* is that it is "on fire." Once the fire is finished with the house, one could say about it, "*La casa se quemó*" since the house itself was damaged by having burned in the fire.

Commands

When you want to get someone to do something, it's best to be polite as opposed to being overly direct, which in the Spanish-speaking world can be mistaken for rudeness. Using the subjunctive mood (which is explained later in this book) is the most polite way. For instance, one could say "Come with me" by saying *Es importante que usted venga conmigo,* which translates to "Its important that you come with me." One could also say, "I need you to come with me" which is *Necesito que usted venga conmigo.* This is the best way to go when speaking in a more formal situation or when you don't know someone very well, where you may want to be more polite. You can even ask "May you come with me?" which can be said as *¿Puede venir conmigo?*

If you want to be quicker and more to the point, which is perfectly fine with people you do know, like family, friends, acquaintances and people who are working for you, then there are two forms that you can use. One is the formal, or *usted* form, while the other is the familiar, or *tú* form. Let's go back to the example, "Come with me." In the usted form, it's *Venga conmigo,* and in the *tú* form, it's *Ven conmigo.* I would save the *tú* command form for people in your generation or younger. Now let's take a look at both forms.

The *usted* form is exactly the same as the subjunctive form. If you want to say "Don't do" something, use "no" in front of the third person subjunctive form of the verb. Here are examples for both below:

(comer)Coma = Eat.....*No coma* = Don't eat.
(irse)Vayase = Go.....*No se vaya* = Don't go.
(correr)Corra = Run.....*No corra* = Don't run.
(venir)Venga = Come.....*No venga* = Don't come.

If you are speaking to more than one person while giving the command, then just add an "n" to the end. For instance, *coma* would become *coman* when speaking to more than one person.

Now if you want to use the *tú* command form, then use the third person present tense singular form for the affirmative commands and the subjunctive *tú* form for the negative ones. Please keep in mind that there are exceptions, like *ir,* that need to be learned. Here are those same verbs from above in the *tú* command form:

*(comer)Come = Eat.....No comas = Don't eat.
*(irse)Vete = Go....No te vayas = Don't go.
*(correr)Corre = Run.....No corras = Don't run.
*(venir)Ven = Come.....No vengas = Don't come.

When speaking to more than one person, I would just stick to the *usted* form, which is what is used in most of Latin America and perfectly understood in Spain. Also, some verbs in the command form are reflexive, like *ir* in the previous example. Another thing to keep in mind, when you have a verb where the *yo* form ends in "go," such as *venir* in the previous example, the *tú* command form shows as follows:

*decir = di/no digas
*hacer = haz/no hagas
*poner = pon/no pongas
*salir = sal/no salgas
*tener = ten/no tengas
*venir = ven/no vengas

Also note that pronouns are added to the command forms. Let's use the verb *dar* as an example. When you want to say "give me," just say *déme*(usted form) or *dame*(tú form). Notice that the pronoun *me* is just added to the end of the verb. And if you want to say "give it to me," then just say *démelo* or *damelo*. The pronoun for the object being given is added after the pronoun of the person receiving the object. If that object is a feminine noun, use *la* instead. Another thing, to say "don't give it to me" is *No me lo dé*(usted form) or *No me lo des*(tú form). Here the pronouns are before the verb. Now here are some other commands(some in the *usted* form, others in the *tú* form) that you may hear and should know in no particular order:

escucheme(listen to me)
no lo haga(don't do it)
cuidate(take care of yourself)
cuenteme(tell me)
hablenos(talk to us)
comala(eat it)
no la coma(don't eat it)
calmate(calm down)
ponlo aquí(put it here)
ven acá(come here)
sientese(sit)
digame(tell me)
no le diga(don't tell him/her)
parate(stop)
tomelo(take it)
no lo tome(don't take it)
hazlo(do it)
ayudame(help me)
levantese(get up)
duermete(go to sleep)
vayanse todos(everyone leave)
olvidatelo(forget it)
miren esto(watch this)

Generally, when it comes to the command forms, it is best to just use the *usted* form. As I've said before, I would only use the *tú* form with children, family(not necessarily with elders), and closer friends. And again, when in a formal situation or when speaking to someone in a position of authority(such as the police), then it's absolutely better to use the subjunctive form as previously discussed.

Comparison

When we make comparisons in English, one thing either has more than or has less than something else. Or it can be that it has as much as something else. In Spanish, there is a template for both. The first one is the *más/menos ......que ......* template. So to say "Your house is bigger than mine," is to say *Tu casa es más grande que mia.* Notice how *más* is before *grande* to mean "more big" or more specifically, "bigger." And for the second part, *que* equals "than." Another example is *Como menos que usted* or "I eat less than you." Notice there is no adjective after *menos.* This is because we are comparing a specific action between two subjects, not comparing two nouns like in the first example. Another thing to note, if you want to compare something to a specific number, *más de/menos de* is the way to go. For instance, if I won more than $1,000 in the lottery, then *yo gané más de 1.000 dólares en la lotería.* If I have less than ten dollars, then I say *Tengo menos de diez dólares.* In other words, *de* equals "than" when comparing to a number. This is all one needs to know when comparing two things in Spanish that are not equal in some way.

For the second comparison, where one thing is as much as something else, use the *tan....como.....* and the *tanto....como.....* templates. Let's start with *tan/como,* which is used with descriptions. So to say, "I can play soccer as well as you," is to say *Yo puedo jugar fútbol tan bueno como tú,* with *tan bueno como* translating to "as well as." Here's another example. *Mi casa es tan grande como tuya,* which is "My house is as big as yours." When saying "as much as" referring to the quantity of something, use *tanto/como* instead. For example, when I want to say that my neighbor makes as much money as me, I can say *Mi vecina gana tanto dinero como yo.* Keep in mind that *tanto* needs to agree in number and gender with the noun in the comparison. Making comparisons in Spanish is pretty easy once you understand how to use these templates.

Corner

There are a couple of words to use here. *Esquina* is the best word when referring to "corner" most of the time, such as the corner of an intersection(or even as the word for intersection itself), the corner of a page in a book, or the corner of a computer screen. However, when referring to an inside corner, such as the inside corner of a room where two walls meet, use *rincón.* So in other words, people meet each other at the restaurant *a la esquina* and then once inside sit at the table *en el rincón.*

Date

In Spanish, date is handled in three different ways. If you are talking about date as in February 15, use *fecha.* If you are talking about going out with someone romantically, use *cita. Cita* would also be used for an appointment with a doctor, dentist or another professional. If you want to say that you have an appointment or meeting and you didn't want to specify further, use *compromiso.* It works well for an excuse such as *Me gustaría ir contigo pero yo tengo un compromiso.*

Drink

Beber is defined as "to drink." *Tomar* can be and is much used in this way as well. So one who drinks milk could say *Bebo leche* or *Tomo leche*. One could also ask *¿Le gustaría beber algo?* or *¿Le gustaría tomar algo?* Both work when asking someone if they want something to drink. Keep in mind, however, that in some places *tomar* can even be used as "to eat."

Drop

There is no one single verb for "to drop," however, it is covered by the verb *caer*. Let's discuss how to use it. If I tell you that you dropped something, then I say *se te cayó*. Here is how we put that statement together. *Se cayó* means that it fell. Then when *te* is added, the meaning changes to that it fell because of you, or that you dropped it. To tell someone what they dropped, you just add what was dropped to the end of the sentence. For instance, *Se te cayó la pelota* means that you dropped the ball. If more than one ball was dropped, then change the sentence to *Se te cayeron las pelotas*. Notice how the verb *caer* matches the number of balls dropped. When I dropped the ball, I would say *Se me cayó la pelota*. If he dropped the ball, then say *Se le cayó la pelota*. These examples are all in the past, if you were holding the ball and about to lose your grip on it, you could say *Se me va a caer la pelota*(I am going to drop the ball). Or if someone isn't being careful with a glass of wine, you could say *Ten cuidado, se te va a caer el vaso de vino*(Be careful, you are going to drop the glass of wine). This concept is relatively easy to handle after some practice.

Enough

Enough is generally covered by a few different words depending on the context. *Basta* or *bastante* are what most Spanish students know and use, however, there are situations where other words would work better. For instance, *suficiente* is a better way to say "enough" as in meeting minimum required. *Bastante* is better for saying "enough" as in plenty. Take a look at the following sentences, *Tengo suficiente dinero por el cine* and *Tengo bastante dinero por el cine.* The first sentence with *suficiente* suggests that you have the minimum amount of money needed without saying if you have any more while the second sentence with *bastante* suggests that you have plenty of money for the movies, or as we would say in English, more than enough. Another example, if a waiter is putting parmesan cheese on your pasta and stops to ask if that is enough, you could respond with *Sí, es suficiente, gracias.* Using *bastante* here almost sounds like the waiter put too much cheese on your pasta dish.

If you are looking to modify an adjective, *bastante* and *suficientemente* work well. They work differently however, with *bastante* meaning plenty and *suficientemente* meaning "just enough." For instance, *Es bastante alto* is "He's plenty tall," maybe even taller than what one was hoping for. *Es suficientemente alto* equates to "He's just tall enough" as in "He'll do." You'll hear *bastante* used this way more often than you will *suficientemente.*
If you are being annoyed by someone, you might yell, "Enough!" or "Enough already!" In Spanish, that is

¡Basta! Or *¡Ya Basta!* Or even just *¡Ya!*

When talking of money, as in having enough to afford something, *alcanzar,* which is "to reach for," definitely works. So you can ask someone if they can afford a new car by simply asking *¿Te alcanza un carro nuevo?* The response you may hear is *Me alcanza* if that person can afford it or *No me alcanza* if he can not.

Fail

Failure is represented by a few words in Spanish. *Fallar* is the most common word for "to fail." If you want to use a stronger word, as in when failing miserably, use *fracasar.* If you are referring to failing an exam, use *reprobar.*

Fear

There are many words used to describe fear. Most of the time in Spanish, you either have fear or something gives you fear. *Miedo* is a general word for fear and the one most commonly used. *Me dan miedo las serpientes* means that snakes give me fear. Meanwhile, *Tengo miedo de las serpientes* means that I have a fear of snakes. Either works for "I'm scared of snakes" or "I fear snakes." They are pretty much interchangeable. A stronger word for fear, such as a phobia, is *pavor.* So if I am really, really scared of spiders, to the point where I can't function when I see one, I can say *Me dan pavor las arañas* or *Tengo pavor de las arañas.* *Terror* can be used here as well and is interchangeable with *pavor.* If I merely want to say that something gives me the creeps, then I can just say *me da cosa.* So if it's spiders, *me dan cosa las arañas.*

If you have a specific fear that something may happen, then use *temor.* An example includes *Mi temor es que ella me odie si le digo la verdad* or "My fear is that she will hate me if I tell her the truth." You can also use the verb *temer,* such as when saying *Temo que ella me deje* for "I fear that she will leave me." And "I fear that you are right" is *Temo que usted tenga razon.* You can use *temo que* for any polite expression that begins with "I fear" in English. Please keep in mind that using *mi temor* and *temo que* requires the subjunctive mood.

If I want to say that you scared me, as in a sudden scare, use *susto.* *¡Qué susto me diste!*(What fear you gave me!) is what you may say when someone jumps from behind a door and yells "Boo!" *Asustar* can be used as *a* verb for "to scare." "You scared me so bad!"(*¡Me asusaste tan malo!*) and "You're scaring me!"(*¡Me estás asustando!*) are good examples. One thing, don't use *asustar* for general fears, only sudden fears. For instance, *Me dan miedo los bichos* means that I fear bugs in general while saying *Me asustan los bichos* leads the listener to believe that the bugs keep coming out of nowhere to harass you.

To say "to scare away," use *espantar.* *El viejo le gusta espantar los niños* works for "The old man likes to scare away the children."

If you want to say that something is scary, just use the noun with *de miedo.* So to say that a movie is scary, just say *Es una película de miedo.* A scary man is *un hombre de miedo* and so forth.

Feel

In English, you can feel something(as in touching something or something touching you) or you can feel like something. If you feel something in Spanish, use *sentir.* To illustrate, if I feel the carpet, then *siento la alfombra.* If Sally feels the sweater, then *ella siente el sueter.* When it comes to how one feels, use the reflexive *sentirse.* So if someone feels sick, *se siente enfermo.* If I feel happy this morning, *me siento feliz esta manaña.* When you feel tired, *te sientes cansado.*

Also, *tener* can be used in this way for certain situations. For instance, another way to say that "you feel tired" is *Tú tienes sueño. Tener* is also used when one wants to say that he or she feels hot or cold. So to say "I feel cold" is *Tengo frío.* "I feel hot" is *Tengo calor.*

If you want to say how something felt when touched, then also use *sentirse.* So when one says that the baby's skin is smooth, she is saying that *la piel del bebe se siente liso.* To say that the blanket feels soft is *La manta se siente suave.* Keep in mind that if I'm just referring to the act of feeling the blanket without saying how the blanket itself feels, then I would just say *Siento la manta.*

If there is a part of your body that is feeling pain, use *doler.* In other words, if I have a headache, I would simply say *me duele la cabeza. Me duele* means that it is giving me pain and the noun, *la cabeza,* is added at the end of the sentence to convey that it is the head that is giving me that pain. If you ask someone if their knee hurts, then you can ask that person *¿Te duele la rodilla?* If I tell you that a woman has back pain, then it is *le duele la espalda.* You can also add *a* *ella* either to the beginning or to the end of that sentence to give further clarification of who is feeling the back pain. *Doler* uses the same pattern as *gustar.*

Now, if I want to say "I feel like," as in to feel like doing something, I could use *tener ganas de* plus the infinitive. "I feel like reading a book" is, for example, *Tengo ganas de leer un libro.* "Do you feel like going to the movies?" is *¿Tienes ganas de ir al cine?* Another thing, if you want to say, "I feel like pizza today" as in having a craving for pizza, you could use the verb *antojar* and say *Me antoja una pizza hoy.* Another example, when asking someone if they feel like or crave french fries is *¿Te antojan papas fritas?* Notice that *antojar* agrees in number with the noun that is craved. Notice that it also follows the same pattern as *gustar.*

Finish

There are two words that are commonly used for "to finish" or "to end," which are *acabar* and *terminar.* Actually, they're synonyms. For instance, if I want to say, "I'm going to finish it later," I can say *Voy a terminarlo más tarde* or *Voy a acabarlo más tarde.* Either would work. If you just want to ask if something is finished, simply say *¿Terminó?* Or even the less common *¿Acabó?*

If you want to convey the meaning of "to finish off," as in using the remaining amount of something, just use *con* after either verb. For example, if I finished off the cookies then I can say *Acabé con las galletas* or *Terminé con las galletas.* Again, either works. The best way to say "to run out of," as in not having anything left of an item, is to use the reflexive form of either verb. For example, "We ran out of money" can either be *Se nos acabó el dinero* or *Se nos terminó el dinero*. If I want to say that I ran out of money, then I just replace *nos* with *me* in that example. If you are in a store and you ask for an item that is no longer in stock, you may just hear *se acabó* for "we're out." *Se acabó* can also mean "it's over" for an event such as a movie or a baseball game.

One very common use of *acabar* that is not covered by *terminar* is "to have just" finished something, which is communicated by *acabar de* plus the infinitive. "I have just eaten," for instance, is *Acabo de comer.* "You have just lied to me" is *Acabas de mentirme. Ella acaba de hacer la tarea* works great for "She just finished the homework." Make sure you know this one.

Fit

Caber is the word for "to fit" found in dictionaries, but *quedar* is used when referring to clothing. To illustrate, *No me quedan estes pantalones* works best when you want to say "These pants don't fit me." If I want to ask you if the shirt fits you well, then I can ask *¿Te queda bien la camisa?* Notice that when the noun is plural, *quedan* is used and when the noun is singular, *queda* is used.

Caber is used for fitting onto or into something. So when I ask if there is any space on the sofa for me, I may ask *¿Quepo yo?* If I want to know if my car fits in the garage, I would ask *¿Cabe en el garage mi carro? "All of the children fit in the classroom"* is *Todos los niños caben en la clase.* That's all there is to it.

Free

In English, free can either mean that something had no financial cost or that there is something available. For instance, you can say that I received an item for free or that I have free time available.

If you want to convey no cost, the word is *gratis*. So if you ask, *¿Cuánto cuesta?* and the answer is *gratis*, well then, put your money away.

If you wish to convey available, then use *libre*. Whenever I want to know if there are any free rooms(as in available) at a hotel, I ask *¿Hay habitaciones libres? Libre* also means "free" as in freedom from oppression of some sort, which could be school, prison, or slavery.

From

De and *desde* can both be used, sometimes interchangeably, sometimes not. It can get very confusing when to use which but there are some general rules to help you get it right most of the time. One rule to go by is to use *desde* when strongly referring to moving from one location or time to another. An example regarding location would be *Corrí desde el parque a la casa* for "I ran from the park to the house." Another example would be someone coming from inside the house such as *Ella vinó desde adentro de la casa.* Or if something was thrown from a moving object I can say *El niño tiró la pelota desde el carro.* An example regarding time is *Desde 1988 a 1998*(From 1988 to 1998). *Desde* is also the word to use for "since." So I can say *No he estado a Disney World desde el año pasado* if I haven't been to Disney World since last year.

Another rule, when referring to where something or someone originated from, without a clear destination, use *de.* So when I say that I am from the United States, I say *Yo soy de Estados Unidos.* To ask someone where they are from, I can say *¿De dónde eres?* If someone took money from your wallet, then *él sacó dinero de tu cartera.* One could also use *de* to say what something was made of or made from. For instance, *Estas botas son de cuero* or "These boots are made from leather." Another way to look at it is that the boots originated from the leather, the same way that I originated from the United States. *El helado es de leche* means that the ice cream is made from milk. So if you use *desde* for "from" when referring to moving from one location/time to another and you use *de* for where something originates from, then you'll be correct most of the time.

Front/Ahead

El frente(not to be confused with *la frente,* which is "the forehead") is defined as "the front" and *al frente de* means "in front of." An example, *El buzón está al frente de la casa* or "The mailbox is in front of the house." *Delante de* can be used in the previous example as well and can also mean "ahead of." That means that if I'm ahead of you in line at the DMV, then *estoy delante de ti. Frente a* is used to imply "in front of" as in "facing" something. If the church faces the plaza, for example, then *la iglesia frente a la plaza.* The phrase *dar a* can be used in the same manner as *frente a,* which makes the previous example *La iglesia da a la plaza.* To say something is up front in a general sense, such as the best seats are up front, then just use *adelante* and say *Los asientos mejores están adelante.*

Funny

In English, funny could mean strange or humorous. If you want the latter, *chistoso, gracioso,* or *cómico* are among your choices. "That is a funny joke" is *Esa es una broma graciosa.* These words are interchangeable except that *cómico* may be stronger.

If you want funny as in strange or weird, *extraño* or *raro* are commonly used. "He's a strange person!" is *¡Él es una persona extraña!* Or it can be *¡Él es una persona rara!* Your choice.

Future

The future can be expressed in a of couple different ways in Spanish. Using the future verb tense is the most obvious one. However, it would be easier in most cases to just use *ir a* plus the infinitive, which translates to "going to" do something in English.

Using this format means that you only have to remember the present tense conjugation of the verb *ir* when speaking of the future. For example, *Voy a comer* works great for "I'm going to eat." And *Ella va a comer* is "She is going to eat." Notice how *comer* doesn't need to be conjugated, just *ir.* You can also convey the future using the present tense, something that is incorrect in English. In other words, there is nothing wrong with saying *Te llamo manaña* for "I'll call you tomorrow." Now, I'm not saying that you don't need to learn the future tense because it is important to know, especially since you would want to understand what is being said when other people are using it, but as you are learning, it may just be easier to stick to the other two ways mentioned above until you become more advanced. Then work the future tense into your speaking.

Guess

Adivinar is the word that covers "to guess," as in "Guess what happened!" or *¡Adivina lo que pasó!* Other phrases we may use include "Guess what!" which translates to *¡Adivina que!* And "Guess who went home!" which is *¡Adivina quien se fue a casa!*

There are a couple of other words to use for guess as well, which are *atinar* and *acertar.* Both of those words are closer to guessing correctly, however. For instance, if your friend asks, "What number am I thinking of? Guess!" You reply, "Seven." Your friend then screams, "You got it!" In Spanish, this would look like:

Friend: *¿De cuál numero pienso? ¡Adivina!*
You: *Siete.*
Friend: *¡Atinaste!*

Acertar is used the same way as *atinar.*

When saying "I guess you can leave" or "I guess we are

here," use *suponer.* Its dictionary meaning is "to suppose," but it works well for the previous examples also, which looks like *Supongo que puedes irte* and *Supongo que estamos aquí* respectively. And if you just want to say "I guess so" as in "I suppose so," then *Supongo que sí* works great. *Supongo que no* is "I guess not."

Half

Medio and *mitad* are both used for half in Spanish. *Medio* is used when looking to say "half of" something. It is used as an adjective. So *media cerveza* is half of a beer and *medio día* is half of a day. When the word "half" itself is a noun, use *mitad.* For instance, to say, "I want half," is *Quiero la mitad.* Or if I want the green half, *Quiero la mitad verde.* If I want half of the pizza, we just go back to using *medio* and say *Quiero media pizza* since I want "half of" the pizza. If I want the half of pizza without sausage, then I would say *Quiero la mitad de pizza sin salchicha,* since the half without sausage is a thing by itself.

La mitad also means "the middle." For example, the middle of the street is *la mitad de la calle.*

Use *medio* when looking to convey "kind of" or "sort of." "I'm kind of hot" is *Tengo medio calor.* "She is sort of ugly" is *Ella es media fea. Un poco* can also be used in place of *medio,* of course, if you just want to say "a little" hot or "a little" ugly instead of "kind of" or "sort of." If you want to respond with "kind of" or "sort of" as an answer to a question, *más o menos* or even *un poco* would work fine. So if someone asks you if the food is good, you could reply with "kind of" or *más o menos* in *español.*

(To) Have Left/Remaining

If you want to say that you have something left or remaining, use *quedar.* For instance, *Me quedan cinco dólares* translates to "I have five dollars left." If I want to say that I have one dollar left, then I would say *Me queda un dólar.* Notice that *quedar* agrees with the number of whatever is remaining. And the pronoun indicates who has whatever is remaining. So if I said that you have five dollars left, then *te quedan cinco dólares.* If we have five dollars left, then *nos quedan cinco dólares. Los niños les queda una hora de la escuela* is "The children have one hour left of school."

Here

Aquí and *Acá* are the words for "here" in Spanish as I am sure you already know. The difference between them is that *acá* is used when the subject is moving and *aquí* when the subject is not in motion. For instance, when you tell someone *venga acá,* the person you are telling to come, the subject, will need to move to come here. If I say that I am here, then I would say *Estoy aquí* since I am the subject who is not indicating movement. That being said, keep in mind that you may still hear Spanish speakers mix them up. Also note that *aquí* may be left out altogether when using *estar.* For example, if someone asked me if my missing brother is here, I could respond with *No está* and leave *aquí* out of that sentence. It's actually quite common to do that. Another thing to note, when being given directions, you may hear *más acá,* which translates to "a little more over here."

A handy phrase to learn for "here you go" is *aquí tiene.* Use it whenever you are handing someone something. So when you hand someone a beer, *aquí tiene.* When the waitress serves your meal, *aquí tiene.*

How

The word for how, as I am sure you already know, is *cómo.* Examples being *¿Cómo comes tan rapido?*(How do you eat so fast?) or *¿Cómo cocinaste el pescado?*(How did you cook the fish?) But if you want to ask how something is or was, never use *cómo,* use *qué tal* instead. For instance, if you want to know how the party was last night, *¿Qué tal fue la fiesta anoche?* If you want to ask how is the game, *¿Qué tal es el juego?* You can even use the shorter and sweeter *¿Qué tal el juego?* Other examples are *¿Qué tal tu carro?*(How is your car?) *¿Qué tal el tiempo en Nueva York?*(How is the weather in New York?) If you just want to ask someone how he or she is doing, then simply ask *¿Qué tal?* This works exactly the same as *¿Cómo estás?*

Parecer is used to ask how one liked something. In other words, if I ask someone how he or she liked the movie, I wouldn't ask *¿Cómo te gustó la película?* I would instead ask *¿Te pareció la película? Cómo* is never used with *gustar* to ask how someone liked something.

If you want to say that someone knows how to do something, just use *saber* plus the infinitive. For instance,

"I know how to swim" is *Yo sé nadar. Ella no sabe manejar* is what you can say if your sister doesn't know how to drive. That's all. No need to use *cómo* in that context either.

Keep

There are a couple of different ways in Spanish "to keep." The reflexive *quedarse con* is used "to keep" possession of an object. *Me quedé con el dinero* works for "I kept the money." *Te quedaste con el dinero* is "You kept the money." If you want to say "Keep the change," then either *Quedate con el cambio* or *Quedese con el cambio* will work fine. *Quedatelo* or *Quedeselo* is perfectly fine for "Keep it."

If you want to convey "to keep" as in keeping something safe, use *guardar,* which can be used to keep an object safe from any number of things. For example, *guardo la leche en la refrigerador* because I want to keep the milk safe from spoilage. If you're married, your wife may ask *¿Me guardas esta bolsa de compras?* Nothing like holding shopping bags so she can buy more stuff for you to hold onto. *Guardar* also gives the context of holding on to something for storage. *José guarda su carro en el garaje* or "Jose keeps his car in the garage."

Mantener is a good verb when "to keep" refers to maintaining. For instance, when I tell my daughter to keep her room clean, I say to her *Mantenga limpio tu cuarto.* And I can say *Me mantengo en buena forma* when I want to let someone know that I keep myself in good shape(which I don't).

If I want to tell someone to keep doing something, as in a command, I can use *seguir* plus the present participle, or -ing form, of the verb. In other words, when I want to say "Keep moving," I just say *Siga moviendo.* And "Keep eating" is *Siga comiendo.* "Keep speaking" is *Siga hablando.* Nice one to remember.

Know

When we use the word "know" in English, it could mean that we know something, as in a fact, such as two plus two equals four, or it could mean that we are familiar with something or someone, such as New York City or Bob. In the first instance, use *saber.* In the second one, use *conocer.* So when I say that I know that Bob is in the United States, I say *Yo sé que Bob está en Estados Unidos.* To say that "Bob knows the United States" is *Bob conoce Estados Unidos.* The first example states that I know as a fact that Bob is in the United States. The second one states familiarity, as in Bob is familiar with and knows his way around the United States. The following examples should clarify further how each word is used differently. *Bob sabe donde Chicago se queda y conoce la ciudad bien*(Bob knows where Chicago is and he knows the city well). *Allí conoce mucha gente*(There he knows many people). *Yo conozco a Bob bien y sé que va a estar bien*(I know Bob well and I know that he is going to be fine).

To use *saber* in conversation, take a look at the following examples. *Yo sé* or *Yo lo sé* works for "I know." "I already know that" is *Ya sé eso.* For "I knew it," you can use *Lo*

37

sabía or for "I already knew it," say *Ya lo sabía* . Keep in mind though that *lo sabía* can also mean that "you knew it" or that "he knew it," so use a subject pronoun like *yo, él, usted,* etc. if the context isn't clear. "I already knew that" is *Ya sabía eso.*

You can also convey the meaning "found out" by using *saber* in the preterite. "I found out," for example is *Yo supé.* "Did you find out when the plane arrives?" is *¿Supiste cuando llega el avión?* If *sabías* is used in place of *supiste,* then the question asks if you already knew when the plane was arriving, implying that you already knew the entire time but didn't say anything.

Now moving on to *conocer.* You can use it in the imperfect past tense to say that you used to know someone. For example, "I used to know Juan" is *Yo conocía a Juan.* If I say *Yo conocí a Juan* then I am saying "I met Juan" as in the first time I actually met him. If I first met Juan in school, then *conocí a Juan en la escuela.* If I say *Yo conocía a Juan en la escuela,* then I'm saying that I used to know Juan when we were both in school, but not necessarily now.

Late

Tarde is the word for late. There is just one thing to keep in mind though. If you want to say someone is late, then use *llegar* in the past tense and not *estar.* So when I'm late, it's *Llegé tarde* and not *Estoy tarde.* "You're late" is *Llegaste tarde. Él llegó tarde* is "He's late." You get the idea. Using *estar* for late is a mistake that many English speakers make but not one that you need to make.

Leave

There are a few ways that we use "leave" in English. One is when exiting or vacating from a place or location. When conveying this message in Spanish, use *salir* or *irse*. Either will work. In other words, "I'm leaving now" can either be *Ya salgo* or *Ya me voy.*

Another way that we use "leave" is when we want to convey leaving something behind. For instance, *Dejé el libro en la mesa* translates to "I left the book on the table." "She left the keys inside the car" is *Ella dejó las llaves dentro del carro.*

One can also use *dejar* for leaving someone alone. So "Leave me alone!" is ¡*Dejame en paz!* You can even just say ¡*Dejame!* by itself. It's the same if you want to tell a bully to leave someone alone. Just say ¡*Dejalo en paz!* or ¡*Dejalo!* Each means "Leave him alone!" Or for "Leave her alone!" use ¡*Dejala!* This works with objects too. So just say *Dejalo/Dejala* whenever someone is touching something of yours that you do not want them to touch. You can also say *dejelo/dejela*, which is the *usted* command form if you want to be more polite.

Like

The word for like, as anyone studying Spanish already knows, is *gustar*. The following examples illustrate how it is used. *Me gusta esta canción* is "I like this song." *A mi hijo le gustan los perros* is "My son likes dogs." "They like ice cream" is *Les gusta el helado.* When I say that I don't like something, I just put *no* in front of the sentence as in *No me gusta esta canción* for "I don't like this song."

If you want to use a word for "like" that is stronger, use *encantar. Encantar* is used for something that you love that is a non-personal object. *Me encanta esta canción* roughly translates to "I love this song." *Encantar* is rarely used for people. Always go with *amar* and *querer* there. So "I love you" is either *Te quiero* or *Te amo.* Keep in mind that *Te quiero* can also mean "I want you" in a sexual kind of way.

Now if you just want to say that you like someone, you can still use *gustar,* but you can also use *caer bien.* "I like my boss," for instance, is *Me cae bien mi jefe.* It translates to "My boss falls on me well" and uses the same pattern for usage as *gustar* and *encantar.* If you want to say "I don't like my boss" you can just add "no" to the beginning and say *No me cae bien mi jefe.* Or you can say *Me cae mal mi jefe.* Both are the same. When I want to say that my boss likes me, I change it around to *Le caigo bien a mi jefe* or that I fall on my boss well. Notice that the *yo* form of *caer* is used here.

One thing to take note of is how we English speakers use "like" for comparisons, such as saying, "He eats like an animal." Use *como* in that instance or *Come como un animal.*

Lo

Understanding this concept will help you sound more natural. *Lo* is used to say "the good thing" or "the bad thing" among other things. To use *lo*, just place it in front of an adjective. Take a look at *lo bueno* and *lo malo,* which are "the good thing" and "the bad thing" respectively. So *Lo bueno es que tengo más plata ahora* is "The good thing is that I have more money now." If I want to say, "The bad thing is that I'm sick," I can just say *Lo malo es que estoy enfermo.* Notice how *cosa* is not used in these sentences. There is no need to put it there. Below are a few other examples:

*lo mejor for "the best thing"
*lo peor for "the worst thing"
*lo extraño for "the strange thing"
*lo único for "the only thing"
*lo chistoso for "the funny thing"
*lo increíble for "the incredible thing"

Also, you can use *es lo* plus an adjective for responses. For example, if someone says that he just passed a test, you can respond with *Es lo bueno que estudiaste*(It's a good thing that you studied). It's a nice little sentence starter.

Lo que

Lo que generally translates to "what" or "that which." It's best to think of it as one word. It typically refers to an object or an abstract idea. Its almost never used in a question. Continue using *qué* in questions. Let's take a look at an example that shows the difference between using *lo que* and *qué* in sentences. If you ask someone "What is he doing?" or *¿Qué hace él?* The listener may reply with *No sé lo que hace* or "I don't know what he is doing." Again, its just *qué* in the question, as it almost always will be, but in the middle of the reply it is *lo que.* The "what" in that reply is in the abstract. He's doing something. So if you put "what" in the middle of the sentence, use *lo que.*

Also, you can start a sentence with *lo que.* For instance, *Lo que pasa* is used when you want to start a sentence with "What is happening." And if you want to say "What you want doesn't exist," then say *Lo que quieres no existe.*

Now, you will see *que* by itself in the middle of a sentence when *que* refers to "that." Take a look at these next two examples showing the difference of when to use lo *que* vs *que.* I know what you want to eat is *Yo sé lo que quieres comer.* If I want to say "I know that you want to eat," then I would say *Yo sé que quieres comer.* Notice the difference. *Lo que* is "what" you want to eat while *que* is "that" you want to eat.

There's another way that we can use this concept. We can use it the same way that we say "the one that's" in English. To illustrate, we can say "My brother, the one that is a doctor, is going on vacation." In Spanish, this can be said as *Mi hermano, el que es médico, va en vacaciones.* Notice that the pronoun before *que* agrees with gender. It will also agree with number. Note the following examples:

Mi camisa, la que tiene huecos, es todavía muy cómoda(My shirt, the one that has holes, is still very comfortable).
Las mesas, las que de madera, son muy bonitas(The

tables, the ones made of wood, are very beautiful).
*_Los árboles, los que vimos en California, son muy altos_(The trees, the ones we saw in California, are very tall).

Look

We use "look" in many ways that are handled differently in Spanish. When you "look for" something in English, you _buscar_ it in Spanish. So when I say, "My wife is looking for her lost keys," then in Spanish I say _Mi esposa busca sus llaves perdidas._

When you "look at" or "watch" something, you _mirar_ it in Spanish. _Miro la televisión_ means that "I'm watching TV." _Él mira esta chica_ means "He is looking at that girl." You can also start a sentence with it as you would in English. _Mire Señor, todavía no tengo el dinero_ is the same as "Look sir, I don't have the money yet."

When you want to say how something looks, _verse_ is good to use. For instance, if I want to ask, "How do I look?" I can say _¿Cómo me veo?_ Or if you want to tell your girlfriend she looks fantastic, just say _Te ves fantástica._

If you want to say "to look like" as in "to resemble," use _parecer._ So to say, "He looks like a soccer player," one would say _Me parece un jugador de fútbol él._ "To look like" as in "to seem" is another way _parecer_ works. _Parece que tu perro está enfermo_ is good for "It looks (or seems) like your dog is sick."

Meaning/Defining

There are a couple of ways to "mean something" with regards to definition. *Significar* works. *Querer decir* is also widely used. They can both be used in the same way. In other words, *¿Qué significa?* and *¿Qué quiere decir?* both translate to "What does it mean?" So "Sprinting means to run fast" is both *Esprintar quiere decir correr rápido* and *Esprintar significa correr rápido.*

If someone says something that surprises you, especially when the news is negative, *Cómo que* is a handy phrase. For instance, if someone says *Estamos perdidos*(We're lost), you can respond with *¿Cómo que estamos perdidos?* (What do you mean we're lost?)

Also, if you realize that you misspoke in the middle of what you were saying, you can use *digo* to begin your correction exactly the way we use "I mean" in English. An example of this would be *Yo vengo a las ocho, digo a las siete,* which is "I am coming at 8:00, I mean 7:00."

Meet

If you want to say that you are meeting up with someone, like in a prearranged social engagement, use *quedar con*. *Quedé con mi novia* is "I met up with my girlfriend." *Juan y yo quedamos con José esta noche al bar* works for "Juan and I are meeting up with Jose tonight at the bar."

If you just bumped into someone without any prior planning, use *encontrarse con*. For example, when I say that I ran into my sister at the movies(without expecting to), in Spanish that is *Me encontré con mi hermana al cine*. If you were trying to avoid Frank but ran into him anyway, you could say *Le trataba de evitar a Frank pero todavía me encontré con él.*

One thing to note is that *conocer* is used for the first time that you meet someone, as explained earlier in this book. For instance, if you met Sarah five years ago for the first time, you can say *Hace cinco años le conocí a Sarah.* If you want to say that we met for the first time at school, just say *Nos conocimos a la escuela.*

Might/May

There is no exact translation for "might" or "may" in Spanish. When referring to a future event, one option is just to start a sentence by using a word for "maybe" with the verb in the present tense subjunctive mood. So you can say *Quizás yo vaya al cine esta noche* for "I might go to the movies tonight." *Talvez comas lo que cocino manaña* is "Maybe you'll eat what I cook tomorrow." *Quizás sea cierto* or *Puede ser que sea cierto* both translate to "It might be true." Other options that can be used are *Es possible que, acaso,* or *a lo mejor*(this one would use the indicative tense of the verb, or just the normal present tense). There are others as well but the key here is to use a version of "maybe."

If you just want to ask "may I" or "may you," use *poder.* Although *poder* is used for "can," in this context, it is also understood as "may." For instance, if I want to ask if I may go to the movies today, then I would ask *¿Puedo ir al cine* *hoy?* If I want to ask someone if they may clean the house I would ask *¿Puedes limpiar la casa?*

Most of

In order to say "most of," the best word to use is *casi.* *"*Most of the time" is *casi siempre,* or literally, "almost always.*"* "Most of the people" is *casi todos.* "Most of the books" is *casi todos los libros.* "Most of the team" is *casi todo el equipo.* Notice the pattern.

Motive

The most common way to say whether or not a deed was done on purpose or on accident is with *con querer* or *sin querer.* Basically if you did something *con querer,* you did it with wanting, or on purpose. And if you did something *sin querer*, you did it without wanting, or on accident. So when I dropped the glass on accident, *Se me cayó el vaso sin querer.* When I scared you with my halloween costume, *Te asusté con querer.*

Move

There are many ways to move around such as walking, running, driving and so forth. The general word for "to move" is *mover.* It's used when not specifying how something moves. For instance, if someone wants you to move a box without specifying how, she may say *Mueve la caja*(Move the box). If you want someone to move, you may say *muevete.* Keep in mind that it may be taken as rude unless you know the person well. *Perdón* or *discúlpeme* probably works better here.

When referring to walking, *caminar* and *andar* are the words found in the dictionary. There is a difference between the two. *Caminar* is used more for the act of walking with a destination in mind or even just the process of walking. *Andar*, on the other hand, is used more for roaming or "to go around." Here are examples showing the differences in how each verb is used. *Camino a la tienda cada día* says that I walk to the store each day. It indicates that I go straight to the store. *Ando por el barrio saludando todos cada día* says that I walk around the neighborhood saying hello to everyone each day. Did you notice that there isn't any specific destination for the sentence with *andar?* I just walk around the neighborhood with no real place to go. *Correr* is used when referring to running instead of walking. *Corro a la tienda cada día* is then "I run to the store each day."

When referring to driving, there are two verbs, *manejar* and *conducir.* So one can say that I drive to work everyday with either *Manejo al trabajo todos los días* or *Conduzco al trabajo todos los días.* There really is no difference. Some regions use one more than the other and vice versa, but you would be understood either way.

When talking about moving into or out of a car, use *subir* and *bajar.* For instance, when I get into the car, *yo subo en el coche*(or *el carro*). And when I get out of the car, *yo bajo del coche.* This works for the bus as well. You'll also hear *suba* when someone tells you to get on the bus and *baje* when someone tells you to get off the bus.

Need

Necessitar is the verb that everyone knows, but another common way of expressing "to need" is *hacer falta.* It loosely translates to lacking something but is commonly used as "to need." If you want to say, in general, that a car is needed, then you can say *Hace falta un carro.* If what is needed is plural, then *hace* changes to *hacen.* For example, *Hacen falta pañales* means that diapers are needed. If one wants to say that the baby needs diapers, then *Le hacen falta pañales al bebe* works. Notice that the pronoun *le* is added to indicate that a third person needs the diapers, which is the baby, indicated by *al bebe. Hacer falta* is good to know since it is used often.

Next

Próximo is the first word most Spanish students learn for "next." There are other words that are better suited for different situations. *Próximo* is still best if whatever is next is indefinite. *Próximo vez* is very common and a great phrase for "next time." However, if you want to say the "next day," *el día siguiente* is much more common. *Próximo* is almost never used in the phrase for the next day, although you'd be understood if you said it. If you say "next week" or "next year" *próximo* may be used but it is much more common for someone to say *la semana que viene* and *el año que viene.* One thing to keep in mind is that *otro* can sometimes be used for "next" as well. It is common in directions. For instance, "the next street" can be *la otra calle* instead of *la próxima calle;* "the next corner" can be *la otra esquina* instead of *la próxima esquina;* "the next stoplight" can be *el otro semáforo* instead of *el próximo semáforo* and so on.

When using next as in "next to," forget *próximo* altogether as it would be absolutely incorrect to use it in this way. *Junto a* or *al lado de* are your go-to options here. So to say that my house is next to the store is *Mi casa está junto a la tienda* or *Mi casa está al lado de la tienda.*

No

There are plenty of ways to say "no" in Spanish so don't limit yourself to just one. You can say "no" more strongly and in some situations, you may very well want to. Some of these stronger phrases include *para nada, en absoluto*(which is more polite) and *ni loco* for "no way." *Eso sí que no* is a fancier way of just saying "no way." If you want to be less polite you can use *En tus sueños* for "In your dreams" or *Estás como loco* for "You're crazy."

Not Anymore

Ya means "now" or "already." In the negative, which is *Ya no*(or you may hear *No ya*), it approximates to "not anymore" or "no longer." So to say that I'm not eating anymore is *Ya no como. Ya no puedo jugar baloncesto* means that I can't play basketball anymore. *Mi hija ya no lleva pañales* means that my daughter doesn't wear diapers anymore. *Ya no* does NOT mean "not yet," which is a common mistake to make. *Todavía no* is best to use for "not yet."

Now

The two words most commonly used for "now" are *ahora* and *ya*. Although *ya* generally means "already," you'll hear it used when someone means "now" as in this very second. An example being ¡*Hagalo!* ¡*Ya!* This translates to "Do it! Now!" I would only use *ya* this way in informal situations when in a hurry since it can come off as rude in the wrong situation. I wouldn't use it with someone who is in a position of authority. *Ahora* should be your go-to word for "now" and you can always use the less abrasive *ahora mismo* or *ahorita* to mean "right now" as opposed to *ya*. To say that you want something done immediately, use *en seguida*. When I tell my family that we need to leave immediately, for example, I tell them *Vamos a irnos en seguida*.

Obligation

Like English, there are several ways to convey obligation in Spanish. One can say that he has to do something, that he should do something, or that he is supposed to do something. If you want to say that you have to do something, use *tener que*. So *Tengo que trabajar mañana* is "I have to work tomorrow." *Tienes que estudiar esta noche* is "You have to study tonight." It can be used for the past also. *Ella tuvé que trabajar ayer así que no vinó* works for "She had to work yesterday so she didn't come."

Tener que is important to understand because it is used for "to have to" all of the time.

You can also say that something needs to be done without stating who needs to do it by using the phrase *hay que*. *Hay que estudiar para aprender* translates into "One has to study in order to learn." Do you see how this is an impersonal statement as opposed to pointing to a specific person having to do something? Another example, *Hay que trabajar para ganar dinero* or "One has to work in order to earn money." This is another handy phrase to know.

If you need to say that someone "should" do something, use *deber* plus the infinitive. For instance, when I say that you should eat dinner before eating dessert then in Spanish I say *Debes comer la cena antes del postre*. And "They should read this book" is *Deben leer este libro*. "I shouldn't go with you" is *No debo ir contigo*. Using *deber* as "should" is pretty straight foward.

In order to convey the meaning of "supposed to," use *haber de* plus the infinitive. "I'm supposed to eat at 1:00" is *He de comer a la una*. "You're supposed to help me today" is *Has de ayudarme hoy*. *Él ha de ir a la escuela esta mañana* is "He is supposed to go to school this morning." It can be and is often used in place of *tener que* as well.

Order

There are a lot of ways that we use order in English that are said differently in Spanish. When looking for order as a noun, well, it can be either masculine or feminine depending on the meaning. *La orden* is the order that you place to your waiter. *El orden* is "the order of things" in relation to their organization or sequence. When you are placing an order, *pedir* is used. "I'm going to order a cup of coffee" is then *Voy a pedir una taza de café.* When you are putting things in order, such as in organizing things, then ordenar is used. So if your friend is getting her life in order, *ella ordena su vida.* Keep in mind that in places where English has a lot of influence, you may hear *ordenar* used the same way as *pedir*.

When you want to order someone around, you *mandar* them. In other words, *mandar* is used when one person orders another person to do something, as in a command. So when my wife told me to wash the dishes, she actually ordered me to wash the dishes, which translates to *Mi esposa me mandó lavar los platos.* If I'm the boss then *puedo mandarle hacer algo a alguien*, or I can order someone to do something.

One thing to note is that when you are looking to just say "in order to" as in to do something, always use *para* plus the infinitive of the verb. For example, *Yo trabajo para vivir* is how to say "I work in order to live."

Para/Por

These two words are among the hardest to get straight for students of the Spanish language. I will provide a framework that will allow you to be right most of the time. Examples will be provided to help you with setting them straight. Now let's take a look at the scenarios where *para* and *por* are commonly confused.

One scenario is when referring to location. In this instance, *para* is used when moving to or toward a specific location and *por* is used when moving through, along or just by a general location. For example, if I say *Manejo para Guadalajara* then I am driving to Guadalajara with Guadalajara as my final destination. If I say *Manejo por Guadalajara* then I am driving by or through Guadalajara. Notice how the meaning of the sentence changes? So if I want to say that I like to walk around Guadalajara, then I can say *Me gusta andar por Guadalajara*. If you use *para*, that could confuse the listener, who may just think that you like to walk to Guadalajara, probably from another city altogether. And if you want to say that the train is going to Toledo, then say *El tren va para Toledo*. If *por* is used here, then it could be mistaken by the listener that the train is just going through Toledo on the way to another destination or even just going in circles within Toledo itself. In short, use *para* when moving to or toward a specific destination and *por* when moving through, around, or along that destination.

Another scenario that confuses people is when substituting the word "for" in English. Let's start with when to use *para* with examples included:

*When a party is the recipient of an object
If I want to tell you that I bought the flowers for my wife, then I would say *Compré las flores para mi esposa*.

*When stating who one works for
If I want to say that my brother works for McDonald's, I

53

would say *Mi hermano trabaja para McDonald's.*

*Deadline
If your teacher says that the homework needs to be completed for tomorrow, then she is setting a deadline. She will probably say *La tarea necesita ser completado para mañana.*

*Comparison
If you want to say, "For a young man, you know a lot," then you can say *Para un joven, sabes mucho.*

Now let's move on to when to use *por* for "for." Here are those examples:

*When there is an exchange or substitution
When two parties make a trade, one object is exchanged for another. So when a brother gives his sister a cookie in exchange for candy, *él le da un galleta por la dulce.* Also, another way to look at it is that the candy is substituting for the cookie. One person substituting for another is also where *por* is used. So if I cook for you, as in I take your place in the kitchen, then *cocino por ti.* If you do my work for me, *trabajas por mí.* Keep in mind that if I am your employer, then *trabajas para mí,* as noted previously.

*Duration of action
Por is used for "for" when referring to how long the action, or the verb in the sentence, lasts. If I work for eight hours every day, then *trabajo por ocho horas todos los días.*

*When searching for an object

Another situation to use *por* is when searching for something. If I go shopping for milk, I am searching for milk to buy, so I can say *Compro por la leche* with *por* representing "for." Keep in mind that if *buscar* is used, it would be incorrect to use *por*, since "for" is included in the verb itself. So the above example would be *Busco la leche.* However, that could mean that you are searching for it in general, not necessarily to buy.

There are additional situations where only *para* or *por* are used depending on what one was attempting to convey. Let's start with the scenarios and examples regarding *para.* One is in regard to an opinion. If you want to say "in my opinion," you could just say *para mí.* To say in Sarah's opinion, say *para Sarah.* So to say "In Sarah's opinion, the flowers are pretty" is *Para Sarah, las flores son bonitas.* Another is when referring to a purpose or goal. So whenever you can put "in order to" in front of a verb, *para* is used. For example, "I study in order to learn" is *Estudio para aprender.* "A lion kills in order to eat" is *Un león mata para comer.* One can also use *para* if the goal is to gain an object. In other words, the previous example with the lion could be stated as *Un león mata para comida,* with food(*comida*) being the object.

Now let's go over situations that require *por.* One scenario is if something is or was done by someone. Therefore a book written by Stephen King *es un libro por Stephen King.* Another situation that *por* is used is for the reason or the cause of an action, such as something happening because of, or on the account of something. Here's an example, *Por José jugaba con los fósforos, ya no tenemos una casa.* In other words, on account of Jose playing with matches, we no longer have a house. Jose playing with matches was the cause of us no longer having a house, therefore *por* is used in front of *José*. Also *por* is used to convey the means by which something is done. As I'm sure you know, the most practical way to travel from New York to Madrid is to fly. In light of that, *yo viajo desde Nueva York a Madrid por avión.* Another reason to use *por* is for unit of measure. When I drive down the highway at 100 kilometers per hour, then *yo manejo cien kilómetres por hora.* And that plane that takes me to Madrid *vuela a casi mil kilómetres por hora,* or it flies at almost one thousand kilometers per hour.

I hope this overview eliminates much of the *para/por* confusion. I know it can be tough to get a hang of, but if you understand this overview you will get *para/por* correct almost every time.

Past Tense(simple)

There are two simple past tenses used in Spanish which absolutely need to be learned. These are known as the imperfect and preterite tenses. One can change the context of the message simply by switching between the two tenses.

There is a way to understand when to use which form most of the time. If we use the English point of view on when to use each tense, it can then be more easily decided which of the two tenses to use. We will use the verb *trabajar* for examples. When you want to say "I worked" at a specific point of time, use the preterite, which is *Yo trabajé.* "You worked" is *Tu trabajaste.* "She worked" is *Ella trabajó* and so on. Basically, when referring to a completed action in English, you would just add the ending -ed, where in Spanish you would use the preterite tense.

Now, if you were to say "I was working," use the imperfect, which in this case is *Yo trabajaba*. "You were working" is *Tú trabajabas*. "She was working" is *Ella trabajaba*. "They were working" is *Ellos trabajaban* and so on. In essence, if someone was in the process of performing an action that occurred in the past with no clear end point, use the imperfect tense. Another time to use the imperfect tense is when you want to convey the idea of "used to." Let's use "I used to work" as an example. "I used to work" is *Yo trabajaba*. "You used to work" is *Tú trabajabas*. "She used to work" is *Ella trabajaba*. So to review, when referring to an action that occurred in the past where there is a clear ending, use the preterite tense. When referring to an action in the past that is continuous with no clear ending, use the imperfect tense. Following this rule will have you using the correct past tense verb conjugation the vast majority of the time.

To break down the imperfect vs. preterite even further, let's go over general rules. The preterite is used for completed actions, especially those with a definite ending point. When it is used, it conveys that an action has already occurred and is over and done with. The imperfect is used when an action is continuous with no obvious start or end point, an action that may still be continuing. It can even be conveyed as a description, as in when providing background information in a story. The examples in the following paragraphs will illustrate the above explanation.

Let's start with the preterite. "I worked yesterday" is *Yo trabajé ayer.* Notice that the action of work ended yesterday and is no longer taking place. And since it is a completed action with a definite end point, the preterite is used. Please consider the next sentence, *Lucía trabajó tarde anoche, luego fue a la fiesta y salió la fiesta temprano.* Here Lucia completed actions in a sequence. She worked late, then she went to the party and finally she left the party early. In order to move on to the next action, the previous one needed to be completed. In other words, before Lucia went to the party, she finished work late, and before she left the party early, she went to the party. Since all of these actions are completed with one action ending as another begins, the preterite tense is used for each verb.

Now let's look at examples with the imperfect. Let's start with *Ella dormía cuando llegaste a mi casa anoche,* which means, "She was sleeping when you arrived at my house last night." *Ella dormía,* or "She was sleeping" is the continuous action, or the background information on what was happening when you arrived, or *cuando llegaste,* last night. You arrived and it was over, while she was sleeping at that time. She could have been sleeping before that time, after that time and maybe she is still even sleeping right now. Look at the next sentence, *Cuando yo era joven, era guapo*, or "When I was young, I was handsome." Here the imperfect is used for both parts of the sentence. The reason being that there is no definite end point for when I stopped being young and when I stopped being handsome. For one thing, people disagree on when one is or is no longer young. Some people will still call me young. The same goes for handsome. It's always best to use the imperfect tense when descriptions are relative. The imperfect is also used to describe habits, or as described earlier, when using the phrase "used to." An example being *Ellos bebían las cervezas todos los días* or "They used to drink beer every day." Please keep in mind that there are exceptions and the above explanations are meant to give a good overview of when to use each of the simple past tenses without getting tangled in the confusing world of grammar. Since the goal is to communicate, I want to stay away from overwhelming you with too many rules that won't come up very often anyway. It's always better to have a basic understanding that you can apply first. You can always refine that understanding later.

Pay

Pagar is "to pay" when it comes to money, but not when it comes to attention. That's because in Spanish, nobody pays attention. Everybody lends their attention. So use *prestar* as it is used in the following example, *Los niños prestan atención a su maestro* (The children pay attention to their teacher).

Piece

There are a few words that you can use here, depending on context. The two most common words for piece are *trozo* and *pedazo*. It is best to use *trozo* when referring to a three-dimensional chunk that is useful in its own right and where there's no distinct division between the part and the whole. A piece of wood, or *un trozo de madera,* is a good example, since it can be broken down into smaller pieces of wood and still be useful. And don't forget, it is still a piece of wood after being broken down into those smaller pieces. Use *pedazo* when referring to something which is not useful in its own right and that has a clear division between the part and whole. A piece of your finger, or *un pedazo de tu dedo*, is a good example, since a piece of your finger is useless if it is not connected to the rest of the finger. It is no longer considered a finger on its own.

When referring to pieces of food that comes in slices, such as pizza, bread, cake and so forth, use *rebanada* although *trozo* is used as well. If you want to ask for a small little piece of something, like a small bite, *nadita* is a cute little word that is also used.

If you want to say "piece" as in a part used in a car, machine or the like, use *pieza*. In other words, a radiator is *una pieza* that may need to be replaced on your car.

Plan

Planear is the word for "to plan." However, other words can be used as well. *Pensar* has "to think" as it's definition but it also works well for "to plan or to intend." So when I say that I am planning on leaving tomorrow, I can just say *Pienso irme mañana.* To say that I have a plan is just *Tengo un plan.* And "to make plans" is *hacer planes. Hago planes para el futuro* is what I would say if I'm making plans for the future.

Play

There are two words that cover "to play." They are *jugar* and *tocar.* Which word to use depends on what is being played. To indicate playing a game, sport or with a toy, use *jugar.* To indicate playing a musical instrument, use *tocar.* Therefore, a soccer player *juega fútbol* while a musician *toca su guitarra.*

Pretty

I'm pretty sure, or *estoy bien seguro,* that you already know that pretty, as in beautiful, is *bonito* or *bello.* But in English, we can say "The man is pretty tall." Here you can use *bien* in place of the English "pretty." It would look like *El hombre es bien alto.* If the sand is pretty hot on the beach, you can say *La arena está bien caliente.* This is a good alternative to *muy.*

Pues

Here is one of the most commonly used words that is very hard to pin down as far as its exact meaning. In fact, it has several different meanings depending on the context. It can be used as a synonym for words such as then, well, so, since, and because, as well as others. You'll hear it more often spoken than you will see it written.

Let's go over examples. If I tell you that I'm hungry or *Tengo hambre*, you may say, "Then eat" or *Pues coma.* If you want to say, "I don't know what to tell you then," then just say *No sé lo que decirte pues.* When using *pues* for "then" in English, it generally indicates a solution, such as in the first example or is a filler word, like in the second example.

Pues is also used in place of an emphatic "well." It is added to provide emphasis to whatever you are saying. For example, if you want to sit down in a chair that was already taken and you want to argue for your right to sit in that chair, the other person may say *Pues, yo llegué aquí primero* or "Well, I got here first." Or if I complained about a bad grade that I received to my mom, she may reply, *Pues, no estudiaste,* or "Well, you didn't study." Another one is *¡Pues claro!* for "Well of course!" Below are other examples where pues is used in place of "well":

Pues sí (Well yes.)
Pues no (Well no.)
Pues, no lo sabía (Well, I didn't know.)
Pues, equivocaste (Well, you were wrong.)
Pues, entiendes la idea (Well, you get the idea.)

In order to indicate cause, where the words because or since are normally used, again, *pues* can be used in place of *porque.* So "I can't walk because I'm drunk" can be *No puedo caminar pues estoy borracho* in Spanish. Also, to say, "I can't drink right now since I have to go to work" is *No puedo tomar ahora mismo pues tengo que ir al trabajo.* Another example, *Digale, pues ella necessita saber eso,* or "Tell her, because (or since) she needs to know that."

Pues can also be used in place of "so" in some contexts. An example is *Querías leerlo, pues aquí está la revista* or "You wanted to read it, so here is the magazine." *Pues* here takes the place of *así que.*

These examples don't show all of the ways *pues* is used, but they do give you a good start on some of the common situations where you will hear it used. I recommend using it as well, since it will help your Spanish sound more natural once you get the hang of it.

Put

In order to say "put" in Spanish, there are two words that are generally used. They are *poner* and *meter. Poner* is used to convey placing something pretty much anywhere, including into or on top of something. *Meter* conveys putting one thing(or things) into something else. So "Put the cookie on the plate" is *Ponga la galleta en el plato.* If you want to say "Put the cookie in the jar," then say *Meta la galleta en el jarro.* But you could still use *poner* there as well. Using *meter*, however, clarifies that the cookie needs to be "put into" the jar since the definition of *meter* is more focused.

Another thing, putting on clothes is conveyed by using *ponerse.* So, if you want to tell someone to put on their jacket, just say *Pongase la chaqueta.* And if I put on my pants the same way as you, then *me pongo los pantalones la misma manera como tú.*

Realize

There is no one word that means "to realize" or "to become aware." *Darse cuenta de* is your best option. Take a look at the following example, *Yo me doy cuenta de que estás cansado*(I realize that you are tired). Here's another example, *Ella se dio cuenta de que llegaste cuando hiciste tanto ruido*(She realized that you arrived when you made so much noise). Notice that she wasn't aware that you had arrived before the noise, but she became aware, or realized, that you had arrived once you made all that noise.

Saber in the preterit tense can also be used, with the meaning being closer to "found out." "I found out that the Cubs won when I was watching the news," for instance, is *Yo supé que los Cubs ganaron cuando miraba las noticias.*

There is also the verb *realizar*, however, it is usually used when turning something into money, specifically cash. For example, *La venta de este carro realizó cinco mil dólares* translates to "The sale of this car realized five thousand dollars."

Really

If someone says something that would prompt a response of "Really?" then just respond *¿De verdad?* You can also respond with "Seriously?" which is *¿En serio?* So if someone told you that the Cubs won the World Series, more than likely, the surprise would prompt you to respond with *¿De verdad?* Or *¿En serio?*

Return

There are two ways that you can "return" from another place in Spanish, *regresar* and *volver.* In other words, I can say *Voy a regresar a casa del trabajo luego* or *Voy a volver a casa del trabajo luego* if I want to say that I'm going to return home from work later. *Mi hijo regresa de México hoy* and *Mi hijo vuelve de México hoy* both work for "My son returns from Mexico today." Either one will work equally well in this context.

If you want to let someone know that you are returning from a place very quickly, as in saying "I'll be right back," there are several phrases that you can use. The most common ones are *Ya vengo* and *Ya regreso*.

Both of these verbs have noun forms as well, *la vuelta* and *el regreso*. So either *A mi vuelta nos vamos* or *A mi regreso nos vamos* works for "On my return we leave." Again, in this context, which phrase to use is up to you.

When referring to returning an object, use *devolver*. For instance, *Ya devuelvo el bolígrafo que me prestaste* means that I've already returned the pen you lent me. If you want to ask your kid if he returned the book to the library, then ask ¿*Devolviste a la biblioteca el libro?* Basically, when a subject is returning an object, use *devolver*.

Now if someone gives me something "in return" for something that I give to that someone, I would use the phrase *a cambio*. So *Te llevo al trabajo cada día si me das dinero por gasolina a cambio* is something I can say if I want gas money in return, or in exchange, for taking someone to work every day. You can use *a cambio* with any exchange.

Same

There can be confusion on whether to use *mismo* or *igual*.

The rule to follow here is to use *mismo* when two or more things are actually the same (person, place, thing, etc.) and to use *igual* when two or more things have some or many of the same characteristics. For instance, if you sit down in a bar and see a random person and then see that exact same person at the grocery store the next day, then *viste la misma persona*(you saw the exact same person). However, if that second person is a close relative to the first person and they share many of the same characteristics, then *te parece son iguales*(they look alike to you but are not the same person). In other words, *mismo* is about identity while *igual* is about appearance and can even be used as equal.

There is another thing to note about *igual*. It can be also used in place of *también*. To illustrate, "me too" can either be *yo también* or *yo igual*.

Save

In English, we save money, save the last donut, and save a life. In Spanish, different words are used for each situation. I *ahorrar* money. She *guardar* the last donut. The doctor *salvar* a life. Here are some examples:

*Ahorro plata para irme en vacaciones(I save money in order to go on vacation).
*Mi esposa guarda el último dónut para nuestro hijo(My wife is saving the last donut for our son).
*El médico salvó la vida de alguien ayer(The doctor saved someone's life yesterday).

Self

When referring to self, *mismo,* which means "same," is the most useful word. So when I want to say that I did it by myself, then I can say *Lo hice por yo mismo.* You can also say *tu mismo* for yourself(*tu misma* when speaking to a female), *él mismo* for himself, *ella misma* for herself, *ellos mismos* for themselves, *nosotros mismos* for ourselves and so on. Notice how *mismo* agrees with gender and number.

Sentence Starters

In English, there are many ways that we start sentences, using words and phrases such as it's that, well, by the way, as well as others. Spanish is no different. Knowing some of these words and phrases will help you better understand what Spanish speaking people are saying and will help your Spanish sound more natural when you use them yourself.

One common sentence starter is the word *bueno.* You will hear it a lot in good spoken Spanish. It is used the same way English speakers use "well." *Bueno, ya voy a la escuela,* for example, means "Well, I'm going to school now." *Pues* is another word to know and is similar to *bueno* when starting sentences. Both can also be used as a crutch word when giving yourself time to think of a response, working like "um" in English. For example, if someone asks you to help them move, you could respond with *Pues(*or *bueno).............me gustaría pero estaré muy ocupado*(Um.........I would like to but I will be very busy). *O sea* can also be used in place of "um."

Another handy phrase with which to begin a sentence is *Es que,* which roughly means "It's that." If, for instance, I asked someone why John is acting weird, I may receive the response "It's that John is drunk" or *Es que John está borracho.* If I follow up with, "Why did John drink so much?" Then I may hear *Es que John no puede dejar de tomar*(It's that John can't stop drinking).

La verdad es que is another way to start a sentence. It roughly translates to "the truth of the matter is" or "the truth is" but can equally be used in place of "actually." If I'm not feeling well and my buddy asks me if I'm ok, I may respond by saying *La verdad es que estoy enfermo.*

One can even start a sentence with just plain old *que.* One way to use *que* when starting a sentence is to use it when answering a question, the same way we use "that" in English, although in Spanish it is used more often. If someone, for example, asks what a sign says, you may respond, "That nobody is allowed to swim in the lake." In Spanish, that would be *Que no se permite nadar en el lago.* It's also used when one repeats himself as well. An example:

Speaker 1: *Voy a trabajar mañana.*
Speaker 2: *¿Qué dijiste?*
Speaker 1: *Que voy a trabajar mañana.*

When repeating a direct command, the subjunctive mood needs to be used as in the following:

Speaker 1: *Vete.*
Speaker 2: *¿Qué?*
Speaker 1: *Que te vayas.*

There are also a couple of phrases to use when one wants to change the subject. One is *En fin,* which equates to "So, anyhow.." It is used to steer a conversation back to its original point, especially if someone has been talking off track for awhile. Another great use for *en fin* is for leading off a concluding thought. Another phrase to use to change the subject, even for no apparent reason at all, is *por cierto.* So if one finds himself in the middle of a conversation having nothing to do with food, he can interject with *Por cierto, ¿Ya podemos comer? Tengo hambre.*

Ser/Estar

Both mean "to be" but are used in different contexts. Anybody who has studied Spanish has learned that *ser* is used when the idea conveyed is more constant or permanent and *estar* when the idea is temporary or changing. Going with that rule will work more often than not but it's also best to know when to use which depending on specific situations including descriptions, location, etc. Let's take a look at those situations.

Descriptions can use either depending on what you are looking to convey. Here are descriptions typically needing *ser.* Notice the examples below:

*El café es caliente.(The coffee is hot.)
*El cielo es azul.(The sky is blue.)
*Nueva York es una ciudad emocionante.(New York is an exciting city.)

Notice that the above examples are general descriptions

that people for the most part regard as true. It's the subject's normal state of being. Use *ser* when making these sorts of statements. If you want to make a description that is different from the normal expectations of people, because of changing conditions, use *estar*. Let's take a look at the previous examples with *estar*. When one says *El café está frío,* what is being said is that a particular cup of coffee is cold when coffee in general is normally hot. Changing the second example to *El cielo está nublado*, or the sky is cloudy, is to acknowledge that normally the sky is blue but for now it is cloudy. To say, in the third example, *Nueva York está aburrida esta noche,* is to say that New York is boring tonight compared to what it usually is. In short, when stating a description that is the norm, use *ser* and when stating a change in condition that deviates from that norm, use *estar*.

There is another thing to consider when deciding between *ser* and *estar*. *Ser* is used with general descriptions, as noted previously, but *estar* also is used when one wants to emphasize that description. For example, one can essentially make the same sentence and replace *ser* with *estar* or vice versa and slightly change the meaning. Take a look at the following examples and notice the difference in meanings depending on which verb is used. *La sopa es caliente* is just stating that soup is hot in general. *La sopa está caliente*, on the other hand, is emphasizing that this particular bowl of soup is hotter than what the speaker expects from soup. Another example is to say that Suzie is beautiful as she always is or *Suzie es bonita.* Meanwhile, if you say that *Suzie está bonita,* then what you are saying is that Suzie is more beautiful than she normally is. Keep in mind that this doesn't mean that she isn't normally beautiful but at this very moment she is extra beautiful. A third example, *El chocolate es dulce* is understood as the chocolate is sweet as always. That is just the main characteristic of chocolate. However, if one says *El chocolate está dulce*, then what is understood is that this chocolate is sweeter than normal chocolate.

Location is served best by *estar* in most instances. For example, if I want to say that I am in Spain then I would say *Estoy en España*. If you are in Panama, then *estás en Panamá*. And if my daughter and I are at the beach, then *ella y yo estamos a la playa*. An exception to this is when referring to an event, in which case, use *ser*. *La fiesta es a la casa de José,* for instance, is "The party is at Jose's house." And to say that the Cubs game is at Wrigley Field is *El partido de Cubs es a Wrigley Field*. Another instance on when to use *ser* is when referring to origin. For example, if I am from Cuba, then *yo soy de Cuba*. And if you are from Miami, then *tú eres de Miami*. The reason for the last two exceptions is that the location where an event takes place and where someone or something originates from doesn't change, unlike the general location of someone or something which can change at any time. Please note the exception of a fixed place like a store or a park still requires *estar*.

When referring to date or time, use *ser*. It is 2:00 is *Son las dos*. If today is Monday, then *hoy es lunes, mañana es martes, y ayer es domingo*. Always use *ser* with date and time.

Occupation is another instance where *ser* is used. So *Yo soy médico* is how to say "I am a doctor." And if my neighbor is a lawyer, then *ella es abogada*. There is no need to use an article like *el/la/un/una* when referring to professions.

Relationships are best served by *ser* as well. Look at these examples:

*Tú eres mi amigo(You are my friend).
*Ella es mi esposa(She is my wife).
*Yo soy tu hermano(I am your brother).

If you want to refer to an action that is in progress, use *estar* plus the present participle tense of the verb(or action) in progress. The present participle tense in Spanish approximates the -ing ending in English. For instance, "I am reading a good book right now" is *Yo estoy leyendo un libro bueno ahorita.* "I'm already working," can be said as *Ya estoy trabajando.* This action tense is only used when the action is in progress. For instance, it's best to say *Estoy nadando a la playa* when I am actively swimming at the beach right now, at this very moment. I wouldn't use *estoy nadando* to say that I normally swim at the beach, as in habitual. For that, it's still *Nado a la playa.* Keep in mind that *Nado a la playa* can be used to state that I'm swimming at the beach currently also, but using the present participle(or -ing) of the verb makes it more clear.

Ser/estar also has its uses when it comes to prices. The rule to follow here is that when you are dealing with prices that are more or less stable, like something you purchase at a retail store, use *ser.* And when dealing with items where prices tend to fluctuate, such as stocks, currencies and the like, use *estar.*

Short

There are two ways to convey short in Spanish depending on what one is looking to say. If you want to say someone or something is not tall, then use *bajo*. An example with *bajo* is *El estudiante es bajo*(The student is short). If you want to say that something is not long, then use *corto*. An example with *corto* being *El cabello de la niña es corto*(The girl's hair is short). Both words need to agree in gender and number.

Sign

We use this word in ways that are said differently in Spanish. Use *firmar* when referring to signing a paper. For instance, *Firmo todos los contractos por mi familia* is "I sign all the contracts for my family." When referring to a street sign, like a stop sign or parking sign, use the word *letrero*. If you want to refer to an intangible sign such as an indication or a signal, use *señal*. *Es una mal señal que te duele el estómago después de comer* is a good example for "It's a bad sign that your stomach hurts after eating." There are other words for this context as well but you will be just fine with using *señal*.

Since

There are a couple of ways to handle this concept depending on what one wants to say. When starting from a point in the past continuing to the present, *desde* is used.

For instance, if you want to say that the dog hasn't eaten since yesterday, just say *El perro no ha comido desde ayer.* To say something hasn't happened since a specific event, use *desde que.* For example, you can say *El perro no ha comido desde que comiste* for "The dog hasn't eaten since you ate."

You may also want to say something like, "Since the dog hasn't eaten, give him something to eat." To do that use *ya que* or *como.* So you can say *Ya que el perro no ha comido, déle algo comer* or *Como el perro no ha comido, déle algo comer.* Either would work. Use *puesto que* if you want to be more formal. Or use *pues* if you wanted to be more informal.

Skip

This one is hard to find in a Spanish dictionary but in most cases "skip" is covered by *saltar* in the reflexive or *saltarse.* So when I skipped class, *yo me salté la clase.* When you skipped breakfast, *usted se saltó el desayuno.* And when your friend skipped a dentist appointment, *ella se saltó la cita dentista.* There are other ways to convey this idea that vary by region but *saltarse* is understood anywhere in the Spanish speaking world.

So

In English, we use the word "so" in many different ways that are covered by different words in Spanish. If you want to start off a sentence with "so," use *así que.* An example would be *¿Así que fuiste a la playa con mi novia?* for "So you went to the beach with my girlfriend?" *Pues* can be used here as well.

Another way to use "so" is to use it to emphasize an adjective. When using "so" in this way, the word you want is *tan.* So to say, "You are so beautiful" in Spanish is *Eres tan bonita.* Other examples include *Este árbol es tan alto*(This tree is so tall) and *Tu perro es tan intelligente*(Your dog is so intelligent). It is very easy to use.

If you want to say "so much" or "so many," then use *tanto/tanta*. *Él tiene tanto dinero* means that he has so much money. Another example would be *Ella ha vivido en tantos lugares* or "She has lived in so many places."

Spend

There are two things that one can spend, time and money. And in Spanish, there is a word for each, *pasar* for time and *gastar* for money. For instance, one who spends their free time in their house in the country can be said in Spanish to *pasa su tiempo libre en su casa en el campo.* But to get there, that same person has to spend money to buy gas, or *tiene que gastar dinero para comprar gasolina.* Either way, it is time and money well spent.

Still

There are a few ways to convey "still" as in "to continue"

or "to keep going" such as *todavía, aún* and *seguir.*
Todavía will work alright as in *Estoy enfermo todavía* for
"I'm still sick." *Aún is* interchangeable with *todavía* and
can also be used in the exact same way as in *Estoy enfermo
aún.*

Yet even another way to say that "I am still sick" is by
simply saying *Sigo enfermo.* Yes *seguir* means "to follow"
but is frequently used as "to continue" also. You can use it
with any adjective. Examples include *Ella sigue
perdida*(She's still lost) or *Sigues joven*(You're still young).
Seguir can also be used with the present participle, or the
-ing form, of verbs. So *Sigo comiendo* works well for "I'm
still eating." Other examples include *Él sigue dormiendo*
for "He's still sleeping." Or *Siguen luchando* for "They're
still fighting."

If you want to say that you still have something, you can
use *seguir con* with a noun. So "I still have a car" can be
Sigo con carro. Of course, *Todavía tengo un carro* works
fine here as well, just more of a mouthful.

In order to convey "still" in the negative, *seguir sin* works
as well as *todavía.* To illustrate, "I still don't believe you,"
can either be *Sigo sin creerte* or *No te creo todavía.* This
works with nouns as well. For example, "I still don't have
a car," can either be *Sigo sin carro* or *No tengo carro
todavía.*

And finally, if you want to convey "still" as in "not
moving," then *quieto* works best. An example being *Me
quedé quieto cuando ví el león* or "I remained still when I
saw the lion."

Stop

There are a few ways to say "stop" in Spanish. *Parar* is the word most associated with stop. "I stopped the car," for instance, is said as *Yo paré el carro.* However, if you want to say, "The dog stopped," as in the dog stopped itself, then you would say *El perro se paró.* So it is reflexive when something or someone stops on its own, as in the example with the dog. It is not reflexive if one thing is stopped by another thing, as in when a person stops the car. *Detener* also works for stop in the same way as *parar.* It is also used for when someone is detained or stopped by the authorities. "I was stopped by the police," for example, is *La policia me detuvo.* In the reflexive, *detener* works the same as *parar.*

Dejar de plus the infinitive is yet another way of saying "to stop" or, better yet, "to quit" a specific action. For example, I can say that I stopped or quit smoking by saying *Dejé de fumar.* And when I say that he stopped eating, I can just say *Él dejó de comer.* And if you just want to say to someone, "Stop that!" then just go with *¡Deje eso!* Or if you are speaking to more than one person *¡Dejen eso!*

Subjunctive(present)

This is a very difficult concept to grasp simply because we don't use it very much in English. Many English speaking Spanish students try to avoid it, however, it needs to be learned in order to speak Spanish well. There are plenty of rules, however, the best way to learn the subjunctive mood at the start is to just learn what triggers it. Gradually, as you practice and use it, the subjunctive mood will become easier to grasp. If you try to learn every rule at the start, you will find yourself too overwhelmed to be able to use it. Besides, once you understand what triggers this mood, you will be right most of the time on when you need or don't need to use it.

In order to conjugate the subjunctive mood, take the *yo* form of the verb and then add the opposite ending to it. Do this for the *yo* form as well as the remaining forms, depending on the ending of the infinitives. So -ar verbs use the -er endings and the -er and -ir verbs use the -ar ending.

Let's start with an -ar verb using *hablar* as the example. Here's how it looks in the subjunctive:
*yo hable
*tu hables
*él/ella/usted hable
*nosotros hablemos
*ellos/ellas/ustedes hablen

Using *comer* as the -er example shows as follows:
*yo coma
*tu comas
*él/ella/usted coma
*nosotros comamos
*ellos/ellas/ustedes coman

And using *vivir* for the -ir verb looks like:
*yo viva
*tu vivas
*él/ella/usted viva
*nosotros vivamos
*ellos/ellas/ustedes vivan

There are also irregular forms but the focus here is to learn the triggers for the subjunctive mood. That way you will know when to use it. There is an acronym that you can use that will help you learn and remember those triggers. That acronym is **WEIRDOS**. Let's go over each letter.

W(wishing, wanting, hoping) is for when the verb in the first clause of a sentence indicates wishing, wanting, hoping, expecting, etc. It indicates uncertainty that the action in the second clause will occur. Take a look at the sentence "I hope that I win the lottery." In Spanish, this is *Espero que yo gane la lotería.* "I hope that" or *Espero que* is the first clause that indicates the uncertainty(since hoping for something to happen doesn't necessarily mean that it will happen) that the action in the second clause will take place. Therefore the subjunctive mood is required. Take a look at some other clauses in this category that trigger the subjunctive mood:
Querer que(to want that)
Desear que(to wish that)
Necessitar que(to need that)

E(emotion) is for a verb indicating emotion. Look at the following sentence, *Me allegro de que estés a la universidad.* Now let's break that sentence down. *Me allegro de que*(I'm happy that) is the first clause indicating the happiness, or the emotion. This emotion then triggers the subjunctive mood in the second clause, *estés a la universidad*(you are at the university). Here are some other emotion clauses that trigger the subjunctive mood in the second clause of a sentence:
Temo que(I fear that)
Me enoja que(I'm angry that)
Me entristezco de que(I'm sad that)

These examples are in the *yo* form because that's how you'll hear them used most of the time, but they can be used in the other forms as well.

I(impersonal observations) is for impersonal expressions that are subjective in nature. They express someone's opinion or judgement on something. It is usually started by *es* plus an adjective plus *que* plus the clause that is in the subjunctive mood. Look at the sentence *Es possible que yo pueda venir esta noche.* The first clause, *Es possible que,* is the impersonal observation that states that it is possible that I can come tonight. This triggers the subjunctive mood because someone else may find it not possible in their observation, which is what makes this statement subjective. Let's look at the next example, *Es importante que tú estudies español.* This is also a subjective sentence, since it is just the speaker's opinion whether or not it is important to study Spanish. Someone else may not think so. It's importance is relative. The first clause is also impersonal, which is why the second clause uses the subjunctive mood in that sentence. Here are some other clauses that trigger the subjunctive mood for this category:

Es probable que(It's probable that)
Es impossible que(It's impossible that)
Es necessario que(It's necessary that)
Es extraño que(It's strange that)
Es chistoso que(It's funny that)
Es bueno que(It's good that)
Es malo que(It's bad that)

R(requesting, recommending, demanding, commanding) is for when the verb is requesting, recommending, demanding, and commanding. It indicates uncertainty since one party requesting or commanding another party to do something doesn't mean that it will happen. As you already know by now, this uncertainty will trigger the subjunctive mood. Take a look at the following examples:

Insisto que te vayas(I insist that you leave).

Pido que me traigas un café(I request that you bring me a coffee).

Vamos a pedirle que venga a la clase(Let's ask him to come to the class).

Recomiendo que probes la langosta. ¡Es rica!(I recommend that you try the lobster. It's delicious!)

D(doubt, disbelief, denial) is for a statement with doubt, disbelief and denial. For example, "I doubt that he will leave" is *Dudo que se vaya* in Spanish. Keep in mind, that if you place "no" in front of the doubting verb, then the subjunctive mood is not used. So the above example then becomes *No dudo que se va*. This is because if there is no doubt, then there is no uncertainty. Also, if you want to say "I don't believe" as the starting clause, you are expressing doubt or disbelief. So "I don't believe that you can do it" is *No creo que tú puedas hacerlo*. *Negar*, or "to deny," is another example. To illustrate, if my brother doesn't want to admit, or denies, that he has the money, then *niega que tenga el dinero*.

O(Ojalá) roughly translates to "god willing" but is used to indicate hope. You can even translate it to "let's hope." Any sentence with this word triggers the subjunctive mood. Here are some examples below:

Ojalá que haga buen tiempo mañana(God willing the weather is nice tomorrow).

Ojalá que no esté allí(God willing he isn't there).

Ojalá que no sigan luchando(Let's hope that they aren't

still fighting).

S(Speculation) is used for when a clause indicates speculation. Speculation refers to things that may or may not occur. Take a look at this example. *Limpie la casa en caso de que venga ella*(Clean the house in case she comes). Notice that it is pure speculation whether or not she comes. We just don't know if she will. Therefore, the subjunctive mood is used. Here are a few other clauses, when used in a speculative sentence as opposed to a factual one, that requires the subjunctive mood:
*a menos que(unless)
**antes/despues de que*(before/after)
*en caso de que(in case that)
*con tal de que(provided that)
*el hecho de que(the fact that)
*aunque(although)
*cuando(when)
*hasta que(until)
*siempre que(as long as)
**tan pronto como, en cuanto*(as soon as)
*una vez que(once you have)

And there you go. Those are the triggers that require the subjunctive mood in a nutshell. Keep in mind that this isn't an all-inclusive lesson, but a way for you to have a good idea of what will generally trigger this mood. Only the present tense subjunctive mood is explained here for purposes of keeping it as simple as possible. Once you understand it, however, the past subjunctive mood will be pretty easy to learn. Just understand that this mood generally expresses how the speaker feels about a possible action or state of being, whether that be uncertainty, doubt or some emotional reaction to something.

Take

"To take" is *tomar* in most instances. There are some exceptions. One is taking someone or something to another location. In that instance use *llevar,* which is defined as "to carry" in the dictionary. In other words, you don't take your kid to school in Spanish, you carry him to school or *llevas a tu hijo a la escuela.* And if you drive your son to school, then just add *en carro* (or *en coche*) which then makes the previous sentence *Llevas a tu hijo a la escuela en carro(coche).* Don't use *manejar* or *conducir* here as Spanish doesn't use metaphors as much as English. For example, "I drive my kid to school" is used in English but *Manejo(Conduzco) a mi hijo a la escuela* is incorrect in Spanish. The initial example using *llevar* and adding *en carro(coche)* is the correct way. You can also add *en avión* or *en tren* or any other way that you can take someone somewhere.

Another exception where "to take" is used by a word other than *tomar* is when there is an object taken out of something. This word is *sacar.* For instance, if I take a cookie out of the jar then *saco una galleta del jarro.* If you take a jacket out of the closet then *saques un abrigo del armario.* You can also use it when referring to people. To illustrate, you can say *¡Sacalo de mi casa!* for "Take him out of my house!" Another one is *Sacame* for "Get me out of here!"

And when you are looking to say "to take off" clothing, use *quitarse. Quitese su ropa* means "Take off your clothes," for example. And if I take off my shirt, then *me quito la camisa.* As you can see, "taking" in Spanish uses several different words, depending on context. Make sure you know each of them as you will hear these words often.

Taking Turns

Taking turns is best said using *tocar.* Take a look at the following to see how it is used. "My turn" is *me toca.* "Your turn" is *te toca.* "Our turn" is *Nos toca.* It uses the same pattern as *gustar*. Asking "Who's turn is it?" is just *¿A quien le toca?* Of course one can just as easily ask "Who's next?" which is *¿Quien sigue?* Also note that *turno* means "turn" as well. So you can say *mi torno* for my turn, *tu torno* for your turn, *su torno* for his/her turn and so forth. *Tocar* seems to be used more often, however.

Talk

There are different words used when referring to talking or speaking. The act of speaking is *hablar,* while *decir* is used to state what is actually said, something I'm sure you already knew. I just want to add that *contar* is commonly used in place of *decir* and is something for which you should be prepared. In other words, if someone wants you to tell them something, you may hear *cuenteme* as often as you would hear *digame.* Another word to be aware of is *platicar.* It can be and will be said in place of *hablar.* *Platicar* is more of an informal word though with its meaning being closer to chatting than it is to speaking.

Tener expressions

There are numerous expressions with *tener* where it has the meaning "to be." In other words, *tener* is used instead of either *ser* or *estar*. Take a look at the most common ones(some with examples) that you should know:

tener frío(to be cold)
-----*Tengo frío*(I'm cold)
tener calor(to be hot)
tener hambre(to be hungry)
-----*El bebé tiene hambre.*(The baby is hungry).
tener sed(to be thirsty)
tener sueño(to be sleepy)
-----*Ella tiene sueño.*(She's sleepy).
tener prisa(to be in a hurry)
-----*¡Tenga prisa!*(Hurry up!)
tener miedo(to be afraid)
tener celos(to be jealous)
tener confianza(to be confident)
tener cuidado(to be careful)
-----*Ten cuidado.*(Be careful.)
tener vergüenza(to be ashamed)
tener razón(to be right)
-----*Tienes razón.*(You're right.)
tener éxito(to be successful)
tener la culpa(to be guilty or at fault)
-----*Lo siento. Tengo la culpa.*(Sorry. I'm at fault.)
tener suerte(to be lucky)
tener lugar(to take place)
tener ganas de(to feel like)
tener en cuenta(to take into account)

tener ___ años(to be ___ years old)
-----*Tiene once años.*(He is eleven years old.)
tener sentido(to make sense)
-----*No tiene sentido*(It does't make sense.)

This is not an exhaustive list, however, these phrases are the most common ones used with *tener.* Notice that with many of them you can use "to have" in English and it will still work. For example, we can either say "I have hunger" or "I am hungry." Although in English you very rarely hear someone say that they have hunger. In Spanish, it is just *Tengo hambre. Estoy hambre* is incorrect. Learn these phrases as they are very useful to have committed to memory.

That/This

If you're reading this book, then I'm sure you already know about *ese, este, esa* and so forth, so we'll skip that part. Here we'll discuss how to say "The house is that big" or "I told you to do it like this." For the first example, use *así de* for "that" as in *La casa es así de grande.* Another example, *Eso niño es así de inteligente* is "That boy is that smart." And for "like that" or "like this," *así* is the best and simplest way as in *Hagalo así* or *"Do it like this."* If someone is doing something exactly the way you want, you can then just say *eso*, which translates to "exactly" or "that's it." Also, if you want to make sure that you are doing something the right way, you may request confirmation by asking "Like this?" which in Spanish is simply *¿Así?* To say "not like this" or "not like that," just say *así no.*

There

There are two primary ways that "there" is used in English, which are when indicating place(*allá, allí* and *ahí*) and when indicating existence(*haber*).

Allá, allí, and *ahí* all mean "there" for indicating place but each has slightly different meanings. Use *allá* when referring to "way over there" such as when something is very far away or out of sight. So, if you're in Mexico and you say "I like it there" when referring to London, you'd say *Me gusta allá.* Use *ahí* when "there" is near the person being addressed. If a girl asks you where to find a book that is located right next to her, you'd point at the book and say *Ahí. Allí* is used when "there" is not near the speaker or the listener. For instance, if you and a friend were walking down the street looking for a third friend, then you finally see that third friend, you may say "There he is!" or *¡Allí está!* One thing to keep in mind, however, is that they often get used interchangeably, even by native speakers, just like *aquí* and *acá* for "here." So if you are struggling to get it right, that's fine, you'll be understood.

Another thing, *allá* is part of a handy little phrase to know which is *más allá.* It means "beyond" or "past." If a taxi driver is driving you somewhere and stops short of your destination, just say *más allá* to have him drive a little further in the same direction. If I am telling you that I live past the school, I would say to you *Yo vivo más allá de la escuela. Más allá* translates to "beyond" in this context. Keep this phrase handy, especially when traveling by taxi south of the border.

When stating that something exists, various forms of the

verb *haber* are used. *Hay* is used to say "there is" or "there are" in the present tense. For instance, if I want to say that there is a clown at the party, I would say *Hay un payaso a la fiesta.* "There are a lot of clowns at the party" changes to *Hay muchos payasos a la fiesta.* Notice how it doesn't matter how many clowns there are, I still just use *hay.* Now take a look at the past tense(there was, there were) with the following example, *Había un payaso a la fiesta anoche,* which translates to "There was a clown at the party last night." *Hubo* can be used as well but *había* is more common. And here's an example when referring to the future(there will be), *Habrá un payaso a la fiesta mañana* or "There will be a clown at the party tomorrow." So, to simplify, there is or there are is *hay.* There was or there were is *había*(or *hubo*). There will be is *habrá.*

Think

This one is covered by two words in Spanish, *pensar* and *creer.* When referring to the thought process or the act of thinking itself, use *pensar. Este libro me hace pensar,* for instance, works for "This book makes me think."

Pensar en and *pensar de* are great for "to think about." They do have a difference. *Pensar en* is for thinking about a subject or topic. *Pienso en políticas todos los días* translates to "I think about politics every day." *Pensar de* is for how you think of something in terms of an opinion. *Pienso buena de tu familia* translates to "I think well of your family." *¿Qué piensas del carro nuevo de él?* asks "What do you think of his new car?"

When thinking is believing, use *creer*. *Te creo* is "I believe you." *Creo que sí* and *Creo que no* are great phrases for "I think so" and "I don't think so." Both are great to have at the tip of your tongue. Use *creame* for "Believe me." *No lo crea* works well for "Don't believe it." *Creo en dios* is "I believe in god."

Time Constructions

Time is communicated in different ways depending on what one is attempting to communicate. When referring to how long it takes to perform a specific task, use *tardar* plus length of time plus *en* plus the infinitive. For instance, *Tardé seis horas en manejar a Miami* would translate to "It took me six hours to drive to Miami." If you want to say it took a while to drive to Miami, substitute *seis horas* with *un rato,* so *Tardé un rato en manejar a Miami.*

Pasar is better when referring to spending time in general. *Pasé seis horas con mi esposa hoy* means "I spent six hours with my wife today." *Llevar* is best to use when describing how long a current action has been taking place. *Lleva dos días buscando una casa nueva* is "She's been looking for a new house for two days." Notice that the present participle of *buscar* is used since the action is still taking place. To say that I haven't slept in two days is *Llevo dos días sin dormir.* You can even use it to ask or say how long something or someone has been somewhere. *Llevo cinco horas a la escuela* works for "I've been at the school for five hours."

If you want to say how long something or someone lasts, use *durar*. *Duré un año en la universidad* or "I lasted one year at the university." You can also use *durar* for how long something is. *La película dura dos y media horas* or "The movie lasts two and a half hours." "How long is the flight?" translates to *¿Cuánto dura el vuelo?*

If you want to say "ago" as in 4 years ago, use *hace.* For instance, *Hace cuatro años, me fui la casa de mis padres* or "Four years ago I left my parent's home." "I ate three hours ago" is *Comí hace tres horas.*

Try

There are three options for "to try." They are *probar, intentar* and *tratar de. Probar* is defined as "to test" but also translates as "to try out." Usually *probar* is used when testing food or drink to see how it tastes but it can also be used with other things such as when trying on clothes to see how they look. Take a look at the following examples:

*Probé el vino, pero no me gustó(I tried the wine, but I didn't like it.)
*¿Puedes probar esta camisa para ver si cabe?(Can you try on the shirt to see if it fits?)
*Probó la silla pero no era cómoda(He tried out the chair but it wasn't comfortable.)

When "to try" refers to an attempt to perform an action, then use *tratar de* or *intentar,* each with the infinitive added. Either works. You can say, for instance, *Trato de beber una copa de vino cada día* or *Intento beber una copa de vino cada día.* Both mean that I try to or intend to drink a glass of wine each day. So, in general, when you "try" a noun, use *probar.* And when you "try" a verb, use either *tratar de* or *intentar.* You will be right most of the time.

Used to

Sometimes you may want to say that you are "used to" something, as in accustomed to it. For this, use the past participle for *accostumbrar.* If I want to say that I am used to the heat, for example, then I can say *Estoy acostumbrado al calor.* If I am used to waking up early, then e*stoy acostumbrado a despertarme temprano.* When referring to a female, use *acostumbrada* as in *Ella está acostumbrada a comer arroz cada día*(She is used to eating rice each day).

When saying that one was "used to" something in the past, *acostumbrarste* is used. For example, *A la universidad, me acostumbré a estudiar tarde cada noche* translates to "At the university, I was used to studying late each night." *Te acostumbraste todos los ruidos cuando vivías en la ciudad* or "You were used to all the noise when you lived in the city" is another example.

If you want to say "used to" as in something that used to happen in the past, use the imperfect past tense. *Yo vivía en la ciudad* is "I used to live in the city," for example. You can learn more about this in the past tense section.

Usually

This concept can be handled a couple different ways. *Por lo general* is best used for generally. For instance,

"Generally, the food is pretty spicy," can be said as *Por lo general, la comida es bien picante.* *Soler* is commonly used for usually as well. "He usually wakes up at 7:00" can be stated as *Él suele despertarse a las siete.* Another example is *Suelo ir a la iglesia los domingos* for "I usually go to church on Sundays."

Waste

Perder, which according to the dictionary is "to lose," is also the best word for "to waste." For example, *perder el tiempo* is to waste time. *Perder una oportunidad* is to waste an opportunity. *Perder una cerveza* is to waste a beer. You get the idea. If you're talking about "to waste" as in "to ruin," then go with *echar a perder.* For instance, *Echas a perder la fiesta* is "You're ruining the party." If you want to talk about waste through food spoilage, then you can use the reflexive *echarse a perder* as in *Coma las bananas antes que se echan a perder*(Eat the bananas before they spoil).

Yes

There are many affirmative answers that you can use in English besides "yes." Spanish has many as well. When we say "of course" in English, *claro que sí* would be said by the Spanish speaker. *Por supuesto que sí* is a little stronger than *claro que sí* and when in a more formal situation, better to use. Both can be shortened to *claro* and *por supuesto.* *Como no* is another way of saying "of course." You'll hear it often. You will just have to get over using the word "no" in an affirmative answer.

If you're looking for an answer that roughly translates to "OK," use *está bien* or even the shorter but more slangy *tá bien*. So when your buddy says that dinner is at seven, you could reply with *está bien* or *tá bien*. *De acuerdo* is a handy phrase that you can use for "alright" or "agreed." If someone asks you to help them move and you agree, you could then reply with *de acuerdo*. *Vale* can be used this same way in Spain. Using more than just *sí* for "yes" will make your Spanish sound less robotic and more natural.

And there you have it! You now have the knowledge to improve your Spanish speaking skills. Now take those skills and use them to take your Spanish to the next level. Immerse yourself! Watch videos and movies in Spanish(stay away from English subtitles as you end up reading them as opposed to listening to the audio). It will help you with your Spanish ear. Don't worry if you don't understand anything in the beginning. It will become easier to understand the more you do it. You can find plenty of Spanish-language videos on sites and apps like YouTube, Netflix, Hulu and others. Also, read books and articles in Spanish. This will help you to reinforce everything that you've learned. And while reading, if you don't understand a word or phrase, see if you can understand what is being said from within the context of a sentence or paragraph before looking up anything. Doing this will help you understand the language better. And last but not least, talk to Spanish speaking people. The back and forth you have in conversations will help you learn to process the language more efficiently because when you have to come up with responses on the spot, you have to think more deeply about the language itself, which in turn allows you to gain a deeper understanding for it. This deeper understanding will lead to the conversations flowing closer to how they already do for you in English. The Spanish language will become more second nature. Again, this will take work and practice, not to mention patience. You just have to go out and do it. *¡Vámonos!*

I would like to thank you again for buying my book. It was a pleasure to write and an even greater pleasure to help you move forward on your journey learning the Spanish language. If you have any questions please email me at jjkozpublishing@gmail.com. You can also follow me on Twitter at @jjkozpublishing if you've enjoyed this book and are interested in anything else that I write in the future. I would greatly appreciate anyone who leaves a review for this book on Amazon. Thank you and good luck!

53736189R00058

Made in the USA
San Bernardino, CA
26 September 2017